JOHN

FOR NORMAL PEOPLE

A Guide through the Depth &
Drama of the Fourth Gospel

by Jennifer Garcia Bashaw

The Bible for Normal People Book Series

JOHN FOR NORMAL PEOPLE

Copyright © 2023 by The Bible for Normal People
Published by The Bible for Normal People
Harleysville, PA 19438
thebiblefornormalpeople.com

Unless otherwise noted, Scripture quotations are the author's own translations. All other Scripture quotations are from the New Revised Standard Version Updated Edition. Copyright © 2021 National Council of Churches of Christ in the United States of America. Used by permission. All rights reserved worldwide.

Library of Congress Control Number: 2023915213

ISBN: 978-1-7364686-6-1 (Print)
ISBN: 978-1-7364686-7-8 (eBook)

Cover design: Tessa McKay Stultz

To the women Bible scholars who came before us, who had to work twice as hard as their colleagues for the respect and success they deserved. You showed us and the world that our voices matter. And to my family who supports and encourages me in every endeavor. I love you.

TABLE OF CONTENTS

Infomercial

Before you read *John for Normal People*, there are ten things you need to know (about me and the book):

1. Hi. I'm Jennifer (or Jen, if you like nicknames). I am going to be a passionate guide in this endeavor because I love teaching the Bible. I have always loved the Bible, albeit in different ways throughout my journey. I remember sitting in church as a child and instead of listening to the sermon, I would read the stories in my pink Precious Moments Bible. I wrote little notes in the margins, sometimes asking questions, sometimes directing comments to God. I was curious and excited to learn more, understand more, and apply more of its messages to my life. My interest only grew as I got older. I was the Goody Two-shoes girl in youth group who looked forward to Bible studies and liked to talk theology (I didn't know to call it that then) with my friends if they would indulge me. College only intensified my obsession. I took quite a few Bible classes at my Baptist university, concurrent with a wide range of English lit classes and that's when I began to study the Bible as literature. Over the course of my study, the naïve view of Scripture I inherited from my Southern Baptist background slowly burned away and I began to deconstruct and reconstruct my theology of the Bible. By the time I finished my Master of Divinity degree, I knew I was going to teach the Bible, either as a minister or as a professor. I eventually chose the professor/PhD path because in my Texas, Southern Baptist context, it was easier for a woman to get a PhD and a teaching position than a senior pastorate. Don't feel sorry for me, though. I love what I do for a living—teaching students and pastors about reading the Bible well, writing about biblical literature, and interpreting the complexity of Scripture for the public with The Bible for Normal People. I humbly offer all my study and my passion to you—the readers of this commentary.

2. The Gospels are my "canon within the canon" and I think they can provide the key to understanding the Bible. You may have heard the term "canon within the canon" before. It means that there is a section of the Bible that you prioritize over others, one that can become a lens through which you see the other parts of Scripture. Most people have a canon within the canon without acknowledging it, so it is better to be honest with yourself and accept that we all play favorites. (Paul's letters tend to be the default canon within the canon for many evangelical traditions, for example, but few admit it). The Gospels are 100% my canon within the canon, partly because their stories transcend time and speak to many generations and partly because they are our main source of knowledge about Jesus—a central way Christians understand the character of God and divine action in the world. As a Christ-centered Christian, I am committed to understanding the message of the Gospels about Jesus and using that knowledge to guide my interaction with the whole Bible, with God, and with human history. So, for me, the better I know the life and teaching of Jesus, the better I will comprehend everything else. That is why I have studied the Gospels on an academic level for twenty-five years now. You might even say I have had an ongoing love affair with the Gospels. The Gospel of Mark was my first love, and I can recall the moment I fell head over heels for it. I was in a class with Dr. David Garland at George W. Truett Seminary and we were acting out the scene from Mark 5 when the shunned and bleeding woman sneaks up behind Jesus to touch the hem of his cloak. I was playing the part of the woman. I can't describe to you exactly what it felt like to immerse myself in the story as a character, but it was perspective-altering. I almost cried when I reached out to touch the person who represented my source of healing. I knew then that I wanted to help other people experience the Gospel stories in the same way I did that day—as visceral, palpable, and transformational. I especially hope to do that with John, because…

3. John is just "built different" than the other Gospels and encourages deep, experimental exploration. I tell my students that although Mark was my first love, John was the one I wanted to settle down with and marry. Yes, I wrote my dissertation on Matthew (sort of by default) and I consider Luke to be my best friend but John is special. It does not tell the story of Jesus the way Matthew, Mark, and Luke do. There is an overwhelming fathomlessness to the Gospel of John that has always intrigued and stimulated me. Unfortunately, its depth cannot be accessed in the way we tend to read it today. In churches, the Gospel of John is read in bite-sized portions, often sucked dry of its original flavor and complexity. Our contemporary experience of John can be like chewing those tiny, dehydrated pineapple chunks in trail mix, but this Gospel was meant to be consumed like a sweet, fresh pineapple—in huge, ravenous bites with the juice running down our chins. I want to give you that juicy, John experience in this book. That is why…

4. This book is a theatrical, updated, and adapted presentation of the Gospel of John. You read that right. I have structured this commentary as a dramatic retelling of the story laid out in John. Instead of dividing the content into biblical chapters, I have separated it into acts (actually, a prologue, four acts, an intermission, and an epilogue). I still tell you what chapters in John we are covering and I stick to the order of John's narrative (with one small exception), but my organization and narration is definitely theatrical. This was done with great forethought to better communicate the impact of the text in its original context. Scholars have long recognized John was read aloud to its first audiences. It reads like an ancient drama, so I have approached the Gospel like a classic play—one that warrants a reimagined revival (how many versions of *Hamlet* have been adapted for screen or stage?). I took this task seriously, studying each passage and its messages to best communicate the original feel of the scene. Since I put so much work into reimagining the story of Jesus for the stage, I ask that you, the reader, keep in mind…

5. This commentary is meant to be experienced, not just read for information. Let's be honest—most commentaries are dry and matter-of-fact. People don't usually sit down and read a commentary from cover to cover because that would be excruciatingly boring. This, however, is not your average commentary. I hope you will read it from cover to cover. My goal is to immerse you in the story of Jesus that John is telling, to connect you to the emotions and events narrated in the text, and to help you better understand how the first hearers of the Gospel of John would have experienced it. I *will* give you information, don't worry about that. You'll get explicit explanations of background issues and academic arguments, plus footnotes that expand on content and point you toward additional resources. But other information will be implicit—for example, the setup of a scene or the flow of a chapter could demonstrate something about the original literary structure. The music referenced may set the tone for a particular passage, orchestrating for a contemporary audience what the original audience would have implicitly understood. What I am saying is, pay attention not just to *what* I write but *how* I write it. Activate your imagination and picture yourself in a theater: feel the excitement in the air, hear the music coming from the pit, open yourself up to the experience of the Gospel. Which reminds me…

6. There are going to be theater staging descriptions and directorial asides in this dramatic commentary. I didn't get fancy about it, but I did want you to be able to picture the staging and motion on stage as I describe it. So, here is a basic guide to stage directions:

Upstage Right	Upstage	Upstage Left
Stage Right	Center Stage	Stage Left
Downstage Right	Downstage	Downstage Left

Apron

Audience

7. Don't be nervous, theater novices are welcome. Not only have I structured this commentary like a play, I have also included a good number of references to plays, especially musicals (which are my favorite). I drop some Broadway allusions here and there and draw examples from theatrical movies. I've even made a playlist for each act. (This will enhance your experience of *John for Normal People*, so please listen to it!) You might be thinking, but I don't like theater…is this book for me? Yes! You don't have to love (or even like) the theater to gain a lot from this approach. I don't particularly care for baseball, but I can appreciate Pete Enns' baseball metaphors in his book, *Curveball*. Who knows? Maybe reading John like a play will awaken your inner thespian. But if not, you'll still be better equipped to appreciate this highly dramatic Gospel when you experience it on its own theatrical terms.

8. We will cover historical background and social and cultural contexts, but our main focus will be on the text itself. Or, to use technical, scholarly language, I will be using some historical-critical methodology in this commentary (my brilliant editors who lean more historical-critical than I do have made sure I included these), but the primary interpretive method I employ is narrative criticism. Narrative criticism focuses on reading biblical texts as literature, using tools from modern literary study as well as ancient literature and dramas. One of the main goals of narrative criticism is to determine what effect biblical stories are expected to have on their audience. This is, in my opinion, the most productive way to study John because it is a complex and beautiful work of ancient literature.

9. A note about translation: you are going to have to trust me. I have gotten creative in the way I have written some of these scenes. Sure, sometimes I quote directly from the NRSVue, but sometimes I use my own translation and often that translation contains a little slang, or an updated idiom, or maybe a bit of paraphrase. Please know that every choice I have made is based on scholarship, my own study, and my desire to communicate the content of John in an accurate and relevant way.

10. This commentary is going to frustrate you at some point. The goal of this book is to help you know and experience the Gospel of John more deeply, not to give you a systematic theology of salvation or a complete picture of Jesus in the Gospels. I will talk about how John is different from the other Gospels and I will highlight the theological statements made in John, but I am not going to indoctrinate you or invent answers to problems that aren't addressed in the text. John does not package everything about Jesus into a pretty box with a bow and it does not tell us how its picture of Jesus is supposed to fit in with the Gospels of Matthew, Mark, and Luke. John is unapologetically con-tradictory to the other Gospels, its metaphors about Jesus are mired with mystery, and its apocalyptic outlook is downright disorienting. But it is also brilliantly descriptive, beautifully dramatic, and so rich in its theological language. I have tried to capture that unique and infuriating beauty in this commentary. So, if you find yourself wanting more as you read *John for Normal People*, if you are frustrated or confused or longing for clearer answers, don't blame me. Welcome to the Gospel of John.

CHAPTER ONE

John from 30,000 Feet

You might have some questions as we embark on this journey through the Gospel of John:

- What exactly is a gospel?
- How historically accurate are the Gospels?
- Why do we have four Gospels?
- Where did John's Gospel come from and why is it so different from the other three?
- What do we learn about Jesus from the Gospel of John?

Well, you are in luck because I am about to answer all of these questions in this introductory chapter (except for the last one because that is the subject of this entire book).

What Is a Gospel?

First things first: the four Gospels—Matthew, Mark, Luke, and John—are the main sources we have that tell us about the life and ministry of Jesus of Nazareth.[1] The genre (or literary type)

---

[1] There are other accounts of Jesus's life written later than the four canonical Gospels—books like the *Gospel of Mary* or the *Infancy Gospel of Thomas* (called apocryphal gospels). These writings are like fan fiction that tell us more about the theological developments of the second and third centuries than about

of the Gospels is different from any genre of writing we would recognize in modern literature. They're actually different from any ancient literature type too, because they comprise a mash-up of different genres. The canonical Gospels display characteristics of ancient historiographies, novels, legends, and biographies. But if you did have to choose one, then the Gospels have the most in common with Greco-Roman "Lives" (*bioi*), a popular style of biography used by historians to memorialize famous leaders. Like these ancient historians, the Gospel writers chose key episodes from their subject's life in order to convey the core of his or her character. They sometimes organized Jesus' words and actions thematically, rather than adhering to a strictly chronological timeline of his ministry. Their narratives highlight Jesus's death, rather than his childhood, because in antiquity, people believed how a person died revealed much about that person's character. Most recently, scholars have also suggested that the Gospels—especially the Gospel of John—favor a particular kind of Greco-Roman biography that made use of *encomium*, a speech that highly praises someone. Encomiastic biographies are like hype literature: their goal is to honor their subject, touting the person's great character and accomplishments (like a eulogy would) and inspiring others to emulate them.

Since Jesus's biographers intended to praise him and his work, it seems appropriate that we would call their writings Gospels, because the word gospel (*euangelion*) literally means "good news." Normally, when someone spoke of "good news" in the Roman Empire it involved Rome's political propaganda; it was used to paint a positive picture

---

Jesus's first-century story. But, boy, are they fascinating! Outside of Christianity, there are also sources that tell us select details about Jesus. The Jewish historian, Flavius Josephus (37–100 CE), mentions that Jesus was a wise teacher who died under Pontius Pilate. The Roman historian, Tacitus (56–120 CE), makes reference to Christians being followers of the man who died at the hands of Pilate as well.

of Caesar's eminence or the superiority of the *Pax Romana*.[2] When the Gospel writers use this term, they are emphatically NOT referring to Roman rule but are describing an alternative to the empire: the reign of God initiated by Jesus. This kingdom was a different kind of kingdom—it was good news for those living on the edges of society, not just Roman citizens who benefited from Caesar's power. The Gospel writers, then, were not merely reporting on Jesus's life—they were retelling the good news about the kingdom Jesus was bringing and convincing their audiences that Jesus's life and accomplishments were worth sharing. In this way, the Gospels might have included a bit of propaganda (not unlike the *euangelion* from which they take their name), but only in the best possible sense of the word.

How Historically Accurate Are the Gospels?

All this talk of genre raises an important question: how historically accurate are the Gospels if their main goal was to praise Jesus and hype up the new way of life he taught? The short (and aggravating) answer to that question is, we can't know for sure. Ancient histories and biographies (even the non-encomiastic kind) valued persuasive description over the presentation of bare facts. It's not that they weren't concerned with truth; it's just that the truths the Gospel writers were concerned with were the deep truths about who Jesus was, why he was important, and why people should follow him…and they did that effectively.

---

[2] The *Pax Romana*, or Roman peace, is the name of a period in the history of the Roman Empire that extends roughly from 27 BCE until 180 CE. This imperial period began with the rule of Caesar Augustus and ended with the death of Emperor Marcus Aurelius. It represents a time of prosperity and political stability for Rome. The empire also used the phrase as a political slogan to boast of their consolidation of power and paternalistic rule over the many people groups within the empire. The irony of the phrase is that the *Pax Romana* was established and maintained by a brutal military force that kept its non-Roman subjects in fear and oppression.

They knew that inspiring speeches and well-crafted stories communicate these truths more successfully than accurate itineraries and lists of places and dates. We shouldn't expect the Gospel writers to follow our modern standards of history and biography—they were ancient people, after all—but we shouldn't assume that they were unreliable witnesses either. They made use of the best literary devices of their time to represent well the person who lay at the heart of their new reality. That was a pretty important job, so you better believe that they took their responsibility seriously and that other early Jesus-followers held them accountable for what their stories taught.

Why Do We Have Four Gospels?

This leads us to another introductory question—if each of the Gospels tell the good news about Jesus's life and ministry, and use similar literary conventions to do so, then why do we need four different Gospels? Wouldn't one be enough? There are multiple reasons the New Testament has four Gospels—the diversity of traditions about Jesus, the unique perspectives each writer provides, and the historical circumstances of the Gospels are all factors. The teachings of Jesus and about Jesus probably went through an oral period for about thirty years after Jesus's death and resurrection. During this time, different communities of Christians told and retold stories of Jesus. Traditions about him spread throughout the churches in the Roman Empire. Finally, when the evangelists began to weave the different oral and written pieces of the Jesus story together, they used numerous snippets of these traditions and patterned these into their Gospels.

Each Gospel writer creates a distinct portrait of Jesus in their story-telling tapestry, emphasizing certain aspects of his character and highlighting what themes and motifs served their audiences best. The writers did not sign their names to their Gospels (any names connected to the Gospels were added later), but we know from the Gospels' content and from some early commentators on the Gospels that the authors did not write at the same time, from the same place, or to the same audiences. They were probably all written in the first century CE, but each had a different provenance, or original background, and slightly different purposes. This is why we have four complementary but diverse stories about Jesus's life, death, and resurrection.

While each Gospel has its own emphases, perspectives, and themes, they also have much in common with one another. Scholars who study the Gospels try to explain the connections between them by looking at their overlapping content and the sources they might have used. When comparing the Gospels, it is clear that Matthew, Mark, and Luke have the most content in common. They follow the same basic plot and timeline, with Matthew adding teaching content like the Sermon on the Mount to the content borrowed from Mark (which is likely the first Gospel written) and Luke expanding the focus and description of Jesus's ministry. Because of the common content between these three Gospels, they are often called the Synoptic Gospels (*syn* + *optic* = seeing together). John, however, is in a league of its own.

Where Did John's Gospel Come From and Why Is It So Different from the Other Three Gospels?

The Gospel of John, sometimes called the Fourth Gospel because of its position in the Bible, has less content overlap with the Synoptic Gospels than one would expect—especially considering they all tell the story of the same man's life. The question of why John is so different from the other Gospels is tied intimately to the questions of John's authorship, date, and origin. So, before we talk about how and why John is different, we need to address some of the background information for John's Gospel. A serious warning first: because the Gospel of John is an ancient document and because ancient people were less concerned with the kind of data we desire today, you will probably be disappointed with this next section. We don't know with any degree of certainty who wrote John, when it was written, or who the original audience was. If you find a commentary online (or a blog or a social media post or a TikTok influencer) that offers confident answers to the background questions we have about John, I recommend you scroll on by. That person has not done their homework, has a very mistaken view of ancient history, and/or has a controlling agenda. We simply do not have solid answers concerning the origins of the Gospels. But, since scholars have tried their best to offer educated guesses over the years and have argued endlessly about the *possibilities* with regard to John's provenance, I will offer some of that interpretive conversation here. But don't get your hopes up.

Let's start with authorship. We have no clarity on whether John was written by one author at one time, multiple authors over stages of time, or a group of people, although all of these possibilities have been suggested. There is a literary reference that might provide a clue to the identity of the author in the book itself: a character called the "Beloved Disciple" (or the disciple whom Jesus loved) who shows up late in John's narrative. This disciple (often referred to by scholars as the BD) is leaning on Jesus's breast during the Last Supper, remains with the women disciples at Jesus's crucifixion, and runs to the empty tomb with Peter. The BD seems to be connected to the authority figure behind the Gospel, and perhaps represents the source behind the stories and vocabulary in John that diverge from the stories and vocabulary we find in the Synoptic tradition. As the epilogue of John reports about the BD in 12:24, "This is the disciple, the witness concerning these things, and the one who has written these things (or caused these things to be written—the verb there can mean either)." Church tradition dating all the way back to the second century CE has identified the BD with John the son of Zebedee, one of the twelve apostles.[3] Modern scholars, however, have suggested a wide array of possibilities

---

[3] Irenaeus makes this claim in 180 CE (as recorded in Eusebius's *Ecclesiastical History* 5.8.4) but his attribution, along with other early Church fathers, seems to be an attempt to connect the Fourth Gospel to a first-person witness, which was an important part of adopting books as authoritative.

for the BD—Mary Magdalene, Lazarus, Thomas Didymus—and some commentators see the character as a literary construct representing an idealized disciple or a group of disciples.[4] One particular strand of interpreters from the 20th century proposed that the BD might represent a whole Johannine community, one that was sectarian in nature and had intentionally split from other forms of Judaism or Christianity in the first century.[5]

Realistically, we don't know who the Beloved Disciple was nor do we know who the author was. But, let's go ahead and move on to the dating of the Gospel and see if there is anything more helpful there. Scholars today mostly agree that John's Gospel was written after the Synoptics, maybe several decades later, mostly because of the theological development apparent in its content (e.g., John presents a Jesus that is more comfortable talking about his connection to the divine, introducing a higher and more developed christology than we see in the Synoptics). Evidence within the text suggests a date after the destruction of the Jerusalem temple by the Romans (70 CE), mainly because the stories in John highlight synagogues over the temple and include several allusions to worship in places other than the temple. The later end of the dating shouldn't extend much

---

[4] Martinus C. de Boer suggests Mary Magdalene as BD in his 1996 *Johannine Perspectives on the Death of Jesus*. Herman C. Waetjen, in *The Gospel of the Beloved Disciple: A Work in Two Editions* (2005), argues for Lazarus as the BD, and James H. Charlesworth defends the possibility of Thomas Didymus as BD in *The Beloved Disciple: Whose Witness Validates the Gospel of John?* (1995).

[5] Scholars have proposed elaborate reconstructions of this hypothetical Johannine community, the various stages of writing, and who exactly was behind the authorship of John (not all believe that the BD represents the community but they do at least suggest a community for the background of authorship). None of these reconstructions can be supported by solid historical evidence, so recent scholarship has moved away from the Johannine community theories, accepting that John's authorship is beyond discovery. But, anyone interested in the most imaginative and influential of these Johannine community theories should check out Raymond Brown, *The Community of the Beloved Disciple* (New York: Paulist Press, 1979).

past the 110s due to the fact that John is mentioned in several second-century sources.[6] This gives John a wide date range from about the 80s to the 110s CE.

When pressed, most contemporary scholars will place John sometime in the 90s CE, so we will assume that general dating here. Not to further complicate things, but it is also possible that John was written in stages by different people or groups of people, with perhaps some chapters being written closer to the time of the Synoptic Gospels and others added decades later. If you sat down to read John from beginning to end, you would notice strange seams, and location and time hops that scholars call *aporias*, that suggest John underwent several stages of composition that were not smoothed out in the final editing process.[7] The 90s CE date, then, refers to the finished Gospel, not the early stages of composition. If the Gospel had been finished sometime in the 90s CE, then the final editors lived through a time period of persecution for Christians, under either the emperor Domitian (who ruled 91–96 CE), Nerva (96–98 CE,) or Trajan (98–117 CE). This period may also have been an era of separation between Christians, who started out as a sect within Judaism, and their Jewish parent faith (a process sometimes called the Parting of the Ways). In short, the Christians who wrote and edited the Gospel of John (as well as its first hearers and readers) would have been experiencing a time of political and religious tension. The shaping and narration of Jesus's life in the Gospel reflects some of that tension and speaks into

---

[6] For example, Basilides of Alexandria quotes John 1:9 in his writings around 130 CE and Justin Martyr mentions Jesus's encounter with Nicodemus around 150 CE. The John Rylands Library Papyrus 3.457, also known as P[52], is a papyrus fragment that contains John 18:31–33 and 18:37–38 on it. It is often dated to the year 130 CE. John likely circulated for decades before these references, so it is unlikely that it was written anytime later than the 110s.

[7] For example, we see Jesus debating with leaders in Jerusalem throughout chapter 5 and then in 6:1, it says, "After this Jesus went to the other side of the Sea of Galilee," as if he had been in Galilee, not Jerusalem. There are several instances of these kinds of *aporias* throughout John.

the late first-century context from which it comes (more on this below when I talk about Elvis).

This brings us to another question that is nearly impossible to answer: where does John come from? Or, to be more exact, in which region of the Roman Empire might the Gospel of John have originated and who was its intended audience (to whom was it addressed and which community first received it)? These questions assume that the authors/editors were from the same geographical area and that they had a particular audience in mind when they composed the Gospel. These are relatively safe assumptions considering the nature of the Gospels, but the caveat is that we should be open to the idea that although the Gospels were written with specific audiences in mind, they were also intended for wider distribution to a more general audience. With that said, let's narrow down the possibilities by looking at the context clues.

Because of the numerous allusions to Israel's Scriptures and Jewish festivals within John, the Gospel's audience likely includes ethnically Jewish Christians. The harsh judgment levied against "the Jews" in John corroborates a Jewish origin—if it were composed for a predominantly Gentile audience, the language would not be as emotionally charged (we'll come back to this intracommunal conflict at the end of this chapter). However, if we place the final dating in the 90s CE, then there would likely have been a mix of Jewish and Gentile Christians in the audience. References to the Samaritans (John 4) and the "Hellenists" (7:35; 12:20) within the Gospel also point to a degree of ethnic diversity. These internal clues don't really narrow down the possibilities for John's origin much, but to humor people who like more concrete answers, here are the top three scholarly answers concerning John's origin (which are more like imaginative suggestions than answers).

Irenaeus, a second-century Bishop in France, locates the origin of the Gospel of John in the community of Christians gathered at Ephesus in Asia Minor. He asserts that John is written to combat a gnostic heresy popular in Ephesus. Since Western-educated scholars tend to love all things early church, and this is a SUPER early source, many of them cite Irenaeus as the gospel truth. However, we must factor in the potential bias of the writer; Irenaeus was, in his own second-century context, combating the gnostic heresy he attributes to John's community. It is more likely that the heresy Irenaeus wrote against was a gnostic *interpretation* of John, rather than a belief that John knew of and refuted at the time the Gospel was written.[8] That doesn't necessarily mean that the Ephesus connection is falsified, but Irenaeus's perceived intent does give some contemporary scholars pause. Outside of this reference, there is not much historical evidence placing the Gospel in an Ephesian context.

The two other popular suggestions for John's place of origin are Alexandria, Egypt (because the earliest manuscripts of John were found there) and Palestine itself (because the author seems geographically familiar with Judea and Galilee). The hard truth that certainty-seekers need to face is that we don't have enough evidence to locate the origin of John's Gospel anywhere specific, and without new archaeological discoveries, we may never have that clarity.

---

[8] Gnosticism is a diverse school of philosophical and religious thought, strands of which influenced some early Christians. The particular brand of gnosticism that Irenaeus combats in his major work, *Against Heresies*, is a gnosticism advocated for by Valentinius, a Christian theologian from the second century (c. AD 100–180). Valentinius taught that there were multiple divine beings called *aeons* that emanated from a supreme God. When one *aeon* named Sophia fell from the divine fullness (*pleroma*), it gave rise to the physical, material world and the *demiurge*, a lesser creator god who was ignorant of the true divine. Some gnostics believed that this ignorant god was the god of the Hebrew Bible. For many gnostics, true salvation from the evil, physical world required gnosis, or enlightened knowledge, that would free a person from the trap of the physical world. Gnostic Christians believed that Jesus was a divine being made human who would lead people to knowledge of the spark of divinity within them. In a nutshell, Irenaeus claims that the Gospel of John refutes these (later) gnostic ideas because it emphasizes that there is one God and one son, Jesus Christ, and denies that secret knowledge is needed for salvation. (Irenaeus, *Against Heresies* 3.1.1–2)

Where we do have clarity regarding John is through what can be observed by reading it alongside the other Gospels. So, let's move on to John's divergence from the Synoptic Gospels. John follows a different timeline and plot than the Synoptic Gospels and makes use of different traditions (or stories) about the life of Jesus. While Matthew, Mark, and Luke present Jesus's teaching in topically arranged parables and sermons, John utilizes private conversations (like those with Nicodemus and the woman at the well) or long speeches (like the Farewell Discourse) to do the same. While the Synoptics recount many of Jesus's miracles, including a decent number of exorcisms, John narrates only seven or eight miracles (which he calls "signs") and does not write about any demon possessions. John lacks several key stories from the Synoptic Gospels, like Jesus's temptation in the wilderness and the pleading prayer in the garden, but he adds a host of new material not seen in the other Gospels. John's new material suggests either that the person (or community) behind this Gospel was unfamiliar with the Synoptic Gospels and used a separate strand of tradition (either written sources or oral) or that the author knew of the Synoptics (probably either Mark or Luke) in some form and deliberately chose to deviate from their stories and perspectives. Scholars have argued for any and every position possible on the spectrum of these two options. The theory that is currently in vogue with prominent Johannine scholars is that John knew Mark's Gospel and echoes some of its teachings and stories but chooses to tell the Jesus story in another way.[9]

---

[9] The argument for John's dependence on Mark is not a new one—early Church commentators posited this. It has experienced a resurgence lately through literary studies on intertextuality. The main reason scholars favor Markan dependence today is because the structure of Mark and John are similar. They both have a John the Baptist beginning, an emphasis on miracles (especially the feeding of the 5,000), and parallel content in the passion accounts. Mark and John share a thematic focus on witnessing and on the nature of the kingdom of God (which John calls "eternal life"). The differences between Mark and John, however, are numerous and scholars usually explain this by suggesting that John made creative and supplemental use of Mark. For more on the connections between Mark and John, see the excellent

You might be wondering, when compared to the Synoptics, how much value does John have for someone trying to reconstruct the historical life of Jesus? Scholars have given different answers to this question throughout history. Many early Christians thought of John as a *spiritual gospel*, focusing on its perspective for understanding the theological significance of Jesus.[10] The fourth-century Christian philosopher Augustine of Hippo summarizes the theological value of John like this: "John spoke about the Lord's divinity in a way that no one else ever did."[11] Respect for the Fourth Gospel's take on Jesus continued through the middle ages but John fell out of favor with commentators when biblical scholarship took a modern turn. The "quests for the historical Jesus," which preoccupied scholars from the 19th century through to the late 20th century, dismissed the Gospel of John as a historical source for the life of Jesus, basing their reconstructions almost exclusively on the Synoptic Gospels.

We may not be able to assess the historical accuracy of John's Gospel, but we do know that it was important to the early church and that the picture of Jesus that it presented was valuable and treasured. People throughout history have come to understand Jesus better, connect with God, and follow Jesus's life example because of this book. We don't have solid answers to the questions modern people ask about John— "When was it written, by whom, and to whom?" or "How accurate are its stories concerning the historical Jesus?"—but what we do have is a well-crafted work of ancient literature written by people who cared to communicate truths about Jesus's life and character.

---

collection of essays in *John's Transformation of Mark*, edited by Eve-Marie Becker, Helen K. Bond, and Catrin H. Williams (London: T&T Clark, 2021). [10] The now-famous phrase, "spiritual gospel," comes from the second-century theologian Clement of Alexandria (recorded in Eusebius, *Ecclesiastical History* 6.14.7). For a deep dive into the early church's interpretation of John, see Bryan A. Stewart and Michael A. Thomas, trans., *John: Interpreted by Early Christian and Medieval Commentators* (Grand Rapids, MI: Eerdmans, 2018). [11] Augustine of Hippo, *Tractates on the Gospel of John* 36.1.

And so that is how we are going to treat John. It is an ancient work of art and we are going to study it as such in this commentary. We are going to ask questions about what the Gospel is communicating and what we might learn from its teaching, but we are not going to pursue questions of historical accuracy. That is like asking how many licks does it take to get to the center of a Tootsie Pop. The world may never know. Since we cannot know what the historical Jesus did or said with any amount of certainty, our path forward involves appreciating the artistry of the Gospel and understanding its momentous claims about Jesus—the Word, who was with God in the beginning and was sent from God to make God known (John 1:1–18). The message about Jesus in the Gospel of John reflects the theology and experiences of some of the earliest Christians. Studying John will help us understand more about why a minority group facing the peril and persecution of the Roman Empire continued to follow and proclaim Jesus as their Messiah and source of life.

How Our Path Will Unfold

Before I lay out the approach of this commentary, it is important for me to share the foundational assumptions about the Gospel of John that undergird our study (note: I have based these assumptions on some of the best and most recent Johannine scholarship out there):

- The mysterious author(s) of John (referred to as "John" or "the authors" from here on) used creative methods to craft a compelling story about Jesus sometime in the late first-century Mediterranean world.

- The purpose of John is to illustrate Jesus's identity and character and to provoke a positive response in its audience. The end of John gives us the key to its purpose: "Now Jesus did many other signs in the presence of his disciples that are not written in this book, but these are written that you may *believe* (or *continue to believe*; the verb form here—*pisteuēte*—supports either of these or both) that Jesus is the Messiah, the Son of God, and that through believing you may have life in his name (John 20:30–31).

- The Gospel of John has historical value, even if it does not present facts in the way we would like it to. It is a dramatic, historical witness to the impact that Jesus made in his context and to the developing traditions in the early church.

- The Gospel of John has a complex relationship to the Synoptic Gospels. Its distinctiveness from them provides a dissonant harmony for us that adds depth to our understanding of who Jesus was to the early Christians.

If you noticed a theatrical tenor to the descriptions I used above—John as a compelling story, as communicating to an audience, as a dramatic witness, as a dissonant harmony—congratulations! You have picked up on the theme of this commentary (or perhaps you just read the title and infomercial). Commentators on the Gospel of John have often compared it to dramas—especially ancient Greek plays and the dramatic readings common in the Mediterranean world. John has a staged flair, with its characters constantly entering and exiting, its long soliloquies, and its cheeky narrator asides. It was written to be performed—read aloud to its audience—and it expected audience participation. So, while John could easily be placed on the library shelf next to Roman biographies, it would also be right at home next to the Greek plays.

John as a Creative Two-Level Drama

For a contemporary parallel, John shares characteristics with biopics and biographical plays and musicals. The 2022 biopic *Elvis* chronicles the rise of one of the most iconic singers in American history. Although the film was based on biographical sources and portrays historical events, the main goal of director Baz Luhrmann was to capture the energy, character, and charisma of Elvis. The film does this well in its retelling of Elvis's rise to stardom, but it reflects the sensibilities and concerns of the 2020s, when it was made, as much as it does the culture of the mid-1900s. Biopics tend to be two-level dramas, commenting on the issues of their present time even as they tell a story about a person from the past. John's Gospel functions in this way. The storyline is set in the 30s CE, during Jesus's lifetime, but it is written half a century later, in the late first century. It is focused on portraying the character of Jesus in a way that also speaks to its current situation. As the authors narrate Jesus's miraculous signs and counter-cultural teachings they address some of the concerns of their late first-century context. As I mentioned earlier, we don't know the exact context of John's audience, but we do see pieces of the narrative addressing issues the audience likely faced: questions about worship (since the temple had been destroyed), situations concerning the inclusion of Samaritans or Gentiles in a Jewish Christian community, and tensions between their community and their Jewish parent faith.

For example, in the story of the man Jesus healed from blindness (John 9), the Jewish leaders interrogate the man's parents about the source of his healing. The parents will not mention Jesus at all, "because they were afraid of the Jews, for the Jews had already agreed that anyone who confessed Jesus to be the Messiah would be put out of the synagogue" (9:22). Scholars deny the possibility of such a thing—if Jesus's followers were ever thrown out of synagogues, it would have occurred much later, when Christianity and Judaism began to split in the late first century. This detail, then, speaks to the context of the Gospel audience, not to Jesus's context. The lines between past and present blur.

We can also see parallels to John's Gospel in modern biographical plays and musicals, which employ creative methods of communication to bring a story to life. In the Tony award-winning musical, *Hamilton*, Lin-Manuel Miranda presents a brilliantly stylized account of the life of Alexander Hamilton. Miranda uses the mediums of hip-hop, R&B,

pop, and soul music to narrate pieces of the Founding Father's history. He also intentionally casts non-white actors to portray well-known white personalities from U.S. history. The musical combines period costumes and historical details with modern lyrics and music styles in order to create its own story world. The result is, in the words of Miranda, "a story about America then, told by America now."[12] With his creative storytelling, Miranda connects his contemporary audience to the past, making the story of an immigrant who had a hand in crafting our country relevant to this moment in history. Miranda's imaginative methods remind us of those we find in John's Gospel. In John, the authors make use of a wide range of artistic devices including dualistic symbolism (light/darkness, life/death, belief/unbelief, etc.), poetry, speeches, dialogues, theatrical scenes, recurring "I am" statements, allusions to Old Testament figures and stories, and a repetitive structure centered on Jesus's signs. We will deal with each of these as we come to them but, for now, know that all these dramatic tools serve to bring the ministry and message of Jesus to life for its audience, just like the hip-hop lyrics and updated casting did in *Hamilton*. John's methods may not be ones we use or understand, but we will try our best to appreciate the first-century context of the Gospel so that we might pick up on the brilliance of John's story world.

The structure of this commentary should help highlight John's artistry and emphases. Because John's goal is to characterize Jesus through his words, miraculous signs, and interactions with other characters, we are going to lean into the dramatic nature of the story. Each chapter will deal with discrete passages as interconnected scenes in a play. Jesus is the main character of almost every scene in John, so we will look at what each scene communicates about his identity and at how other characters in the scene enhance Jesus's characterization or teach us something about "the world." I have arranged the scenes into acts and they are as follows:

---

[12] Edward Delman, "How Lin-Manuel Miranda Shapes History," *The Atlantic* (September 29, 2015).

THE PROLOGUE: JOHN 1:1–18

Overture & Origin Story

JESUS

The Word | The Light | The Life | The presence of God in the flesh tabernacling among us

SUPPORTING CHARACTERS

God, the Father | John (the Baptist) | The World | Those who accept the Word and those who reject the Word

ACT 1: JOHN 1–4

The Messiah Makes His Debut

JESUS

The Lamb of God | Rabbi | Son of Man | Son of God | King of Israel | Holy Spirit Baptizer | Messiah

SUPPORTING CHARACTERS

Jesus's first disciples | Jesus's mother | Religious leaders and crowds | Nicodemus | The woman at the well | The royal official and his household

ACT 2: JOHN 5–8

Jesus: Love Him or Leave Him

JESUS

Son of the Father | The Son of Man who will judge the world | The prophet (who is to come into the world) | The Bread of Life | The Light of the World

SUPPORTING CHARACTERS

Religious leaders | The man healed by the pool | Jesus's family members | The crowds | The disciples who stay and the disciples who go

INTERMISSION & BONUS SCENE

ACT 3: JOHN 9–12

Light, Life, & the Pursuit of Salvation

JESUS

Son of Man | The one who gives sight to the blind | The Good Shepherd | The Gate | The Resurrection and Life | The Way

SUPPORTING CHARACTERS

The man healed from blindness | The man's parents | Mary, Martha, and Lazarus | The divided crowds | Caiaphas and Jewish authorities | The disciples

ACT 4: JOHN 13–20

The Final Countdown

JESUS

The Self-giving Servant | The Glorified one | The Spirit giver | The Scapegoat

SUPPORTING CHARACTERS

Jesus's mother and the other women | The Beloved Disciple | Mary Magdalene | Thomas | Peter and the other disciples

THE EPILOGUE: JOHN 21

A brief note about characters and perspective before we proceed: almost all of the characters in John are Jewish people in a first-century context. Some will be portrayed in a positive light by the authors and some will have negative titles and characteristics assigned to them. Scholars have not figured out all the nuances of John's portrayal of Jews. However, it is clear that there are negative feelings expressed about some of the Jewish characters in the story. We must be careful to view these characters and their literary descriptions as part of the story world, and not as legitimate assessments of the Jewish people or Judaism. Too many people throughout history have used the negative depictions of the character group called "the Jews" in the Gospel of John to discriminate against Jewish people, to persecute Jewish individuals, or to promote anti-Jewish and anti-Semitic violence in the world. Please be aware of that as you experience this complex piece of literature.[13]

Final note: I have structured this book/theatrical endeavor so that you become a part of the audience for the drama that will unfold. The other audience members are those first-century hearers of John who experienced the Gospel in their Mediterranean context. Some of the directorial choices and narrational asides are for them and some are for you. I have frequently blurred the lines between past and present for exegetical purposes but, let's be honest, for entertainment value as well. So, if you are ready to experience the Fourth Gospel in a new and exciting way, alongside its first audience, go ahead and use the restroom and then make your way to your seats. The show is about to begin.

---

[13] If you find yourself wondering about the negative portrayal of Jews and Judaism within the Gospel of John, I would encourage you to check out R. Alan Culpepper and Paul N. Anderson's collection, *John and Judaism: A Contested Relationship in Context* (Atlanta, GA: SBL Press), 2017 or Adele Reinhartz's book, *Cast out of the Covenant: Jews and Anti-Judaism in the Gospel of John* (Grand Rapids, MI: Fortress Press), 2018.

CHAPTER TWO

The Prologue: John 1:1–18 Overture & Origin Story

CHARACTERIZATIONS OF JESUS

The Word | The Light | The Life | The presence of God in the flesh tabernacling among us

SUPPORTING CHARACTERS

God, the Father | John (the Baptist) | The World | Those who accept the Word and those who reject the Word

---

The cast is assembled and the lights start to dim. Before the curtain rises—while you are still settling into your plush and springy velvet-covered chair—the orchestra starts to play what sounds like a mashup of songs. That's the overture: an introductory number comprising short snippets from the show's most iconic songs or chord progressions that repeat throughout the score, hinting at the emotions and themes to come. The overture serves as a preview for first-time showgoers, but for those who are already familiar with the score—who have listened to the soundtrack over and over—the overture is a reminder of everything they love about the musical. It primes fans so that they are thrumming with excitement before the curtain even opens. The prologue of John functions very much like an overture. For first-time readers, it introduces themes and characters to come, foreshadowing conflict and plot points. And for those who have already encountered John? Well, for us, it strikes chords of emotion deep within us, causing us to anticipate the way Jesus's story is going to make us feel, even though we've read it time and time again.

And yet, John's prologue does even more than introduce the coming story. It's kind of like the first song of the musical, *Hamilton*, aptly titled "Alexander Hamilton." That opening number does operate like an overture, patching together key phrases and musical refrains that will appear in later songs, but it also serves as Hamilton's origin story, dynamically contextualizing the main character and where he comes from. Through its lyrics, we learn of the hardships Hamilton faced growing up in poverty on a Caribbean island...

> How does a bastard, orphan, son of a whore/And a Scotsman, dropped in the middle of a forgotten spot/In the Caribbean by providence impoverished/In squalor, grow up to be a hero and a scholar?

...and the journey he takes to work his way to America. John's prologue is Jesus's origin story. It provides background information about the Gospel's main subject and serves as an introduction to the complex identity of The Word (the Logos), otherwise known as Jesus Christ.

The Prologue as Jesus's Origin Story

In ancient Hebrew literature, the first appearance of a character is important. Authors craft the introduction to a main character carefully, hinting at what role the person might have later, foreshadowing their successes and failures. A good example of this is found in 1 Samuel: when we first meet Saul in the narrative (1 Sam 9), he is described as tall, rich, and handsome but the introductory story about him relates how he was looking for his father's donkeys and could not find them. (As I tell my students: he couldn't even find his own ass!) In contrast, when we meet David (who is also described as handsome), he is anointed by Samuel and the spirit of the Lord comes on him. His first action in the story is to play soothing music on his lyre for Saul, who was being tormented by an evil spirit (1 Sam 16). These introductions foreshadow the characteristics of both David and Saul and set the tone for the plot of the story, in which Saul displeases God, goes crazy, and loses the throne while David gains favor with God and people (at least for a while).

Each of the Gospel writers, who were raised reading ancient Jewish literature, take great care to introduce Jesus in ways that point to his significance and hint at both his background and his future. Mark's intro is the most terse and to the point—he does not even mention Jesus's birth or early life. His Gospel starts, "The beginning of the good news (*gospel*) of Jesus Christ," and then he immediately quotes from the prophet Isaiah about John the Baptist (Mark 1:1–3). From the get-go, the audience is to understand that Jesus is the Christ (a.k.a. the Messiah), his story is a good news announcement (like the birth announcement of an emperor), and his ministry is connected to the tradition of the Hebrew prophets through John the Baptist.

Matthew and Luke add more detail when introducing Jesus, and begin their accounts before his birth, setting the stage for his appearance. Both provide human origin stories, but weave the supernatural throughout their infancy narratives. Matthew begins with a genealogy that connects Jesus with the Davidic throne and points to the universality of his ministry through the inclusion of foreign women. Then the birth narrative begins: Joseph, a salt-of-the-earth Jewish man finds out his betrothed is pregnant—and not by him—but he decides (after a persuasive visit from an angel) to marry her, rather than divorce or stone her. The birth of the baby captures the notice of Eastern astrologers and also causes consternation for King Herod, the paranoid despot in the land. Eventually, Jesus gets some gifts from the magi before the young family flees to Egypt to escape Herod's deadly temper tantrum.

Matthew's introduction to Jesus highlights his human roots and the dire circumstances of oppression he is born into—complete with a tyrant's rule, a family fleeing as refugees, and the death of innocent babies. Matthew's genealogy of Jesus works together with the story of the Eastern pagans to show that Jesus's impact would extend beyond Jewish religious folk to reach across gender, ethnic, and religious boundaries. Matthew also wants us to notice Jesus's divine beginnings, including a virgin birth, visits from angels, and supernatural dream warnings.

In Luke's Gospel, we see Jesus's origin story through the eyes of Mary, a poor girl from Nazareth who becomes a prophet, the proto-disciple, and the *theotokos* (bearer of God). She sings a song about the nature of God and predicts the trajectory of Jesus' ministry (see the Magnificat in Luke 1:46–55), and then gives birth like a boss in less-than-ideal conditions. Also making appearances throughout Luke's birth narrative are singing angels announcing peace on earth and humble shepherds who are the first humans to hear about the birth. Luke also includes a genealogy, one that traces Jesus back to Adam, linking him with all humanity.[1]

Though they differ in the details, Luke and Matthew's origin stories serve similar purposes, connecting Jesus to the rich history of Israel (and humanity), emphasizing his mundane, earthly begin-nings, and incorporating divine activity acceptable to their Jewish audiences (angels, dreams and the work of God's Spirit). All of this works together to characterize Jesus as both the savior of the world and a human, born in poverty like many Jewish people under the rule of the Roman Empire.

And then we come to John's introduction to Jesus...

---

[1] Note that while Luke traces Jesus's genealogy back to Adam, Matthew traces it back to Abraham. This is not the only difference between Matthew and Luke's genealogies, but I will leave further discussion to the future authors of *Matthew for Normal People* and *Luke for Normal People*.

John is not as subtle as the other Gospel writers about Jesus's divine origins. John's Gospel foregoes a human genealogy and a charming story about betrothals and stables. John locates Jesus's inception not in a woman's womb, but in the very word and person of the divine. For John, Jesus was not merely announced by angels and conceived by the Holy Spirit, he was active with God at creation and was a part of the divine being:

In the beginning **the Word** was,
> And **the Word** was with God,
> And **the Word** was God.[2]
He was present with God in the beginning.

All things through him **came to be**.
> And not one thing **came to be** without him;
> What has **come to be** in him was life,
And the life was the light of human beings.

And the light shines **in the darkness**,
> and the darkness did not grasp it.[3]
> > (John 1:1–5, translation mine)

---

[2] There has been some argument about whether the word for God at the end of verse 1 should be translated as "a god" or "divine" instead of "God" because there is no article attached to the word in Greek (or, as we like to say in the biz, it is anarthrous). In the Septuagint (the Greek version of the Hebrew Bible), the word is used both with and without an article to refer to God. So the grammar can sometimes be ambiguous. However, the grammatical construction here, the poetic repetition the author employs—the word was, the word was with God, the word was God—and the fact that this is an introduction to the theme of Jesus and the Father being one all suggest that the translation is "God". With that said, I don't think it's a good idea to base the entire doctrine of Jesus's divinity on one poetic passage.

[3] The word used here, *katalamanein*, which I have translated "grasp," is notoriously difficult to translate. It could mean "to comprehend" or "to welcome/

Is John's Prologue a Hymn? A Poetic Introduction? A Bridge?

Scholars have argued over the literary form and purpose of John's prologue for centuries, but have not arrived at a conclusion. Even if I hadn't divided the above verses into strophes, it would still be pretty obvious that the first lines of the prologue are poetic. If you continue reading into verse 6, though, you would see that the song-like quality of the prologue pauses. Verse 6 sounds like the introduction to a folk tale:

"There once was a man sent from God whose name was John…"

Okay, the word "once" isn't in the Greek but you get the picture. After the section on John-sent-from-God, the prologue slips back into a rhythmic pattern in verse 10. The point is that yes, there is poetic form in John 1:1–18, but it is mixed in with prose. For all its beauty and depth, it is a Frankenstein of a passage. So interpreters of John, even from the earliest centuries of Christianity, have had a hard time agreeing on the original form or boundaries of the prologue. I am including 1:1–18 as the prologue just because I am not really a boat-rocker and that is what most of your Bibles will say.

The background of the prologue is also in doubt. Some suggest it was originally a separate hymn sung to the Word in early churches. If this is the case, the hymn was probably adapted for use as an introduction and incorporated into John, maybe with additions pieced together with the John the Baptist material in 1:6–9 and 1:15.

---

receive" or "to overtake, overcome"—and each of these meanings communicates something different. We may not have to choose just one meaning, though. Scholars suggest that the author may be using a multi-faceted word like "grasp" to convey several meanings at once (like a double entendre without the risqué element). In that case, the darkness in the world did not understand or receive the light, something we learn later in the Prologue, and it also did not defeat or overcome the light.

But this is not the only possibility: because the themes of the prologue fit so well with the body of John's Gospel, it may have been composed specifically to serve as a poetic introduction to the story, either by the primary authors of John or a later editor. The prologue may also function like a musical bridge connecting the lyrical verses of the Hebrew Bible (the diverse stories they tell of Israel and their God) to the next part of the faith song, Jesus's ministry and the birth of a new faith community. So, what I am saying is we cannot know for sure the nature of the prologue or its relationship to John's Gospel, but we can treat the prologue as it appears in its final form in our biblical texts as an introduction of sorts to the Gospel. It has enough vocabulary and themes in common with the rest of the story that we can safely assume it is connected.

The Prologue and Creation

The prologue is not only connected to the story of the Gospel; it is connected to the story of Israel's Scriptures. Notice that the prologue starts out just like Genesis does: "In the beginning." To be more accurate, the prologue uses Genesis 1:1 as it appears in the Septuagint.[4] The parallels do not end at "In the beginning." The words and themes in the Genesis 1 creation account appear throughout the verses of John's prologue.

---

[4] The Septuagint (the Greek version of the Hebrew Bible) was the primary version of Scripture Jewish people living in the first century would have used. Greek was the lingua franca of the time (the Latin of the Roman Empire had not caught on yet) and although scribes and their students would have been able to read Hebrew, Jewish writers usually quoted from the Greek text. But the Septuagint was not an exact translation of the Hebrew Bible; it had extra verses and its own phrasing, creating discrepancies between the Hebrew and Greek, so it is often easy to tell the difference between the two when a New Testament author quotes from Israel's Scriptures.

Connection to Genesis 1 Creation Account	
John 1	**Genesis 1**
In the beginning (1:1)	*In the beginning God created the heavens and the earth...*
The Word	*Then God said... (1:3, 6, 9, 11, 14, 20, 24, 26)*
In him was life	*Creation of living creatures (1:20), of humankind (1:26)*
The light shines in the darkness	*God separated the light from the darkness (1:4)*

These connections serve several purposes. First, they help the audience identify the Word as a part of God's act of creating. Some commentators would say that the prologue here makes the Word an agent of creation or a force active in creation—"All things through him came to be. And without him not one thing came to be" (1:3). The connections also forge a link between the beginning of the Hebrew Bible and the beginning of the story of Jesus. It is common in John for the authors to make reference to the Hebrew Bible, to Jewish religious traditions, or to the story of God and Israel, placing Jesus's story firmly in his ancient Jewish context.

Lastly, the thematic parallels to the Genesis 1 account of creation provide essential context for the main character from the prologue: the Word. The Word as a character could be influenced by Greek philosophy—the *logos* for philosophers like Aristotle was a principle of logic, encompassing other characteristics such as reason, wisdom, and order. However, if we refer to the chart with the Genesis parallels, it becomes apparent that the thought world of the Hebrew Bible provides the simplest and best context for understanding the Word. The Logos is, as the parallels show, the creative word of God, which brought all things into being. We learn in John's prologue that this divine Word is not only the initial life-giving force behind creation, it is also the light that "shines in the darkness" (1:5)—in other words, the *ongoing* divine work in the world. This light is what will overcome the darkness or—cue bass note ominously reverberating through the theater—any other force that may come against it.

The Prologue as Overture: Anticipating the Themes

With that bass note hanging in the air, it's time to look at how the prologue works like an overture, introducing and foreshadowing some themes and main ideas that appear later in the Gospel. There are several motifs the prologue mentions that will become key in John's narrative world. Just looking at the first prose section about John the Baptist (1:5–9), we see four themes foreshadowed: the light/darkness motif, the description of being sent from God, the centrality of witness or testifying, and the importance of belief. Or, to use some quick-reference words that would each make excellent songs in the Gospel of John musical I might one day write: Light, Sent, Witness, Believe.

Light

John 1:5 portrays the Word as a light—"And the light shines in the darkness, and the darkness did not grasp (*comprehend and/or overcome*) it." A couple of verses later, the prologue contrasts John, the witness to the light, with the Word, who is "the true light which enlightens everyone" (1:9). These verses provide a glimpse at a key motif in John— the opposing forces of light and darkness. As we saw in the last chapter, John's Gospel makes ample use of dualism. In this dualism, Jesus is associated with light while forces that are opposed to Jesus are characterized by darkness. Case in point, John 9:4–5 has Jesus making the statement,

> "We must work the works of the one who sent me while it is day; night is coming, when no one can work. As long as I am in the world, I am the light of the world." (Translation mine)

Another direct reference to light/day and darkness/night comes in Jesus's advice to his disciples in chapter 12:

> "The light is in you for a little longer. Walk while you have the light, so that the darkness may not overtake you. If you walk in the darkness, you do not know where you are going. While you have the light, believe in the light, so that you may become children of light." (12:35–36, NRSVue)

John similarly uses night and day as thematic backdrops in his narrative: Nicodemus comes to Jesus at night, implying not only his covert mission but his lack of understanding; Jesus meets the woman at the well in the middle of the day, demonstrating the enlightening nature of their conversation and her acceptance of the messiah; and Judas leaves to betray Jesus in the night, sketching a scene of opposition and misunderstanding. The reference to light and darkness here in the prologue is the first mention of this motif, and it lays the ground rules for the later references—Jesus is light and those captive to darkness will have a hard time comprehending and accepting him, but they will not stop (overcome) his mission.

Sent

In 1:6, the prologue describes John the Baptist as "a man sent from God." The idea of someone being "sent" reverberates through this Gospel (to the tune of 60 times!), but it starts here with John the Baptist. Following is an overview of the major senders and sendees, roughly in the order they appear in the narrative.

(1) God Sends John (the Baptist) Here in 1:6 and also in 1:33 and 3:28, John speaks of God as the one who sent him to baptize and the one who sent him ahead of Jesus. It is fascinating that the next time John uses the word "sent" it is to describe Jesus (see 3:34) and...wait for it...it is right after John says in 3:30, "He must increase but I must decrease." So, as the focus moves firmly from John's role in the story to Jesus's role, the language about the one being sent shifts to Jesus.[5]

(2) The Father Sends Jesus The identification of Jesus being the one sent from God is so pervasive in John's Gospel that I cannot exhaustively list every instance. The following examples show that the idea of Jesus as the sent one pops up frequently, often in reference to Jesus's role or relationship to God, and mostly as dialogue from Jesus's mouth:

- "My food is to do the will of the one who *sent* me and to complete his work." (Jesus in 4:34)

- "Anyone who does not honor the Son does not honor the Father who *sent* him." (Jesus in 5:23)

- "And this is the will of him who *sent* me, that I should lose nothing of all that he has given me but raise it up on the last day." (Jesus in 6:39)

- "I will be with you a little while longer, and then I am going to him who *sent* me." (Jesus in 7:33)

- "Whoever believes in me believes not in me but in him who *sent* me. And whoever sees me sees him who *sent* me." (Jesus in 12:44–45, all NRSVue)

---

[5] John the witness and baptizer (he is not called "the Baptist" in John's Gospel) plays an important role in the Jesus story, especially here and in Mark. The authors of John's Gospel portray him as a herald or messenger sent in the same way the prophets were sent, and the movement he initiates is influential. In the prologue, he takes on the role of someone known to the audience, who then points to Jesus as being greater than himself. John the Baptist is mentioned favorably in the writings of the Jewish historian Josephus, so it is likely that he was well-known and respected by first-century Jews. Some scholars note the replacement language used in the Gospel of John indicates there were still followers of John the Baptist when the Fourth Gospel was written, so the language of this Gospel de-emphasizes him to focus on Jesus.

Okay, okay, you get the point. There are many other references to Jesus as one sent by the Father in John—so many, in fact, that it would be safe to say that it is the central identity marker for Jesus in this Gospel. Jesus himself says it *ad nauseam*, but the narrator also comments in a key passage about Jesus's sent-ness: "Indeed, God did not **send** the Son into the world to condemn the world but in order that the world might be saved through him" (3:17, NRSVue). Folks who grew up in church might think of Jesus as the one who loves or who heals or who sacrifices, but we must recognize that in John, Jesus is definitively the one *sent from God*. And there is more to this idea of being sent: Jesus is not simply a courier or a gift being sent. If you go back and look at the list above, the "sent-ness" of Jesus reveals another truth about him—he does the work of God and shows people the will of God. Jesus is sent to be the light and the representation of the Father on earth.

(3) Jesus Sends the Disciples and the Spirit Jesus is not the only one sent in John's Gospel. Jesus also talks about sending his disciples in the same way God sent him. In his prayer for the disciples in John 17, Jesus tells God, "As you have sent me into the world, so I have sent them into the world" (17:18, NRSVue) and right before he breathes the Spirit on them post-resurrection, Jesus tells the disciples, "As the Father has sent me, so I send you" (20:21, NRSVue). The Spirit is also sent, although it is a bit unclear who exactly sends the Spirit. In chapter 14, Jesus tells the disciples that the Paraclete (Advocate), or Holy Spirit, "whom the Father will send in my name, will teach you everything and remind you of all that I have said to you (14:26, NRSVue). Here, the Spirit is sent from the Father. In the next chapter, the sending action shifts a bit: "When the Advocate comes, whom I will send to you from the Father, the Spirit of truth who comes from the Father, he will testify on my behalf" (15:26, NRSVue). Here, *Jesus* is going to send the Spirit but the Spirit is still from the Father. Finally, in 16:7, Jesus speaks of the Advocate coming to them, but only if Jesus goes away: "If I go, I will send him to you."

Jesus is clearly doing the sending in this verse. So, John is either giving mixed messages about who sends the Spirit or he is moving the source of sending gradually and purposely from the Father to Jesus to connect Jesus and God more deeply. Regardless, the Advocate is sent as well as Jesus, and it seems the Spirit serves as the continuation of Jesus's work in the world on behalf of God.[6]

Witness

I mentioned earlier the strange, folktale introduction of John the Baptist. In this prose section, the prologue introduces yet another key concept from John's Gospel—the importance of witnessing or testifying. John (sent from God) "came as a *witness* to testify to the light, so that all might believe through him" (1:7, NRSVue). The author is careful then to point out that John "himself was not the light, but he came to *testify* to the light" (1:8, NRSVue). Just as the concept of sent-ness is central to the thought world of John's Gospel, the idea of witness—testifying or declaring the identity of Jesus—is central to the plot. As soon as the prologue ends, our witness to the life of Jesus (the Gospel author) introduces the witness of John the Baptist into the story and after that, it is testimony after testimony from Jesus's disciples about who Jesus is. It is a brilliant literary device. The author uses the witness of the people from the narrative as breadcrumbs dropped to tell us more about who Jesus is and to lead us to greater understanding about his identity.

---

[6] A note about the pronoun used for the Holy Spirit: the Spirit does not have gender. However, English translators will use the pronoun "he" for the Paraclete in John because the Greek word *parakletos* is masculine. Unfortunately, many translations also use "he" in the other Gospels when the word used is *pneuma*, which is a neuter (non-gendered) word. This is a reflection of how Christianity has made its language for God exclusively masculine, using male pronouns for God, Jesus, and the Holy Spirit despite the fact that God and the Holy Spirit are not gendered.

Believe (Trust!)

Another key plot element introduced in the prologue is perhaps the most famous theme from John—belief. If you grew up in the evangelical movement, or even in close proximity to it, you probably have John 3:16 memorized. "For God so loved the world that he gave his one and only son that whoever *believes* in him will not perish but will have eternal life" (I used all the masculine pronouns for nostalgia—let's not forget that God is not male!). Belief in Jesus is the stated purpose of the Gospel of John—"But these are written so that you may come to believe (or continue to believe) that Jesus is *the Messiah, the Son of God*" (20:31). The word translated as "believe" here carries the idea of faith—putting your faith in someone—or trusting. It is an active idea, not just a passive assent or an academic exercise. After each miraculous sign that John reports (those signs that form the structure of the first half of the Gospel), people are said to either believe/trust in Jesus or to reject/oppose him. This central theme of belief is laid out in the prologue in two places: in 1:7 where John "came as a witness to testify to the light, so that all might *believe* through him" (NRSVue) and in 1:12, where the author states, "But to all who received him, who *believed* in his name, he gave power to become children of God" (NRSVue).

A Sneak Peek at the Characters and Coming Action

Let's recap before we bring this number home. The prologue serves as an overture, introducing snippets of the coming themes, and functions like the origin story for Jesus, introducing who he is and where he comes from. There is one more role the prologue plays and the aforementioned "Alexander Hamilton" can help us with this as well. *Hamilton*'s opening song introduces the audience to some of the main players in the story: each delivers musical lines that provide a sneak peek into their relationship to Hamilton, foreshadowing later events in the play. We learn about fellow soldiers Lafayette and Hercules Mulligan ("We, fought with him"), about his connection to Washington ("Me, I trusted him"), about his wife Eliza and other love interests ("Me, I loved him") and, finally, the climactic event of the musical, Aaron Burr's deadly duel with Hamilton ("And me, I'm the damn fool that shot him").

John's prologue provides a similar sneak peek. It introduces the main characters of the story—God, the Word, John, those who accept the Word and those who reject the Word. Note how 1:10–13 illustrates what the rest of the Gospel will go on to narrate—that Jesus would be rejected by his own people but some would receive him:

> "He was in the world, and the world came into being through him, yet the world did not know him. He came to that which was his own, and his own people did not accept him. But to all who received him, who believed in his name, he gave power to become children of God, who were born, not of blood or of the will of the flesh or of the will of man, but of God." (NRSVue)

These verses introduce a theme that manifests like a character in the story, the world. Starting here, John will present a multi-valent picture of the world—the world does not "know God" (7:28, 8:55, 15:21, 16:3, 17:25), and is associated with darkness (1:5, 12:46), but is still loved by God and can be rescued (John 3:16–17). It is not completely clear who or what the authors mean by "the world" because it is a shifting metaphor. Sometimes "the world" refers to people who resist Jesus's message, but other times "the world" seems to include all people plus the created order. Because the prologue begins at creation, we should assume that the whole cosmos is in view for some of these passages (perhaps in "God so loved the world…").[7]

---

[7] For more on "the world" as a character in John, see Cornelis Bennema, *Encountering Jesus: Character Studies in the Gospel of John*, 2d ed. (Minneapolis, MN: Fortress), 2014.

The prologue also lays out some insider information about the Word—information that other characters in the story will not have or understand until the end. See how many insider tidbits the author introduces in this pivotal and concluding section of the prologue:

> And the Word became flesh and *tabernacled* among us, and we have seen his glory, the glory as of a father's only son, full of grace and truth…From his fullness we have all received, grace upon grace. The law indeed was given through Moses; grace and truth came through Jesus Christ. No one has ever seen God. It is God the only Son, who is close to the Father's heart, who has made him known. (1:14, 16–18, my translation)

We learn from these dense, deeply theological lines that the Word became incarnate (en-fleshed) and that his presence among his people was God's presence. The word sometimes translated as "dwelt" has a close kinship with the Greek word for tabernacle, the movable tent that housed the presence of God among the Israelites. We also hear that the Word is the Father's only son, that he is greater than John the Baptist, that we will receive grace from him, that he will continue the work of Moses and the law, and that the Word is Jesus Christ (verse 17 is the first mention of Jesus the Messiah!). Then, the last sentence of the prologue tells us the most important bit of information about the Son, giving us the key to understanding this Gospel and Jesus's life and ministry: Jesus, who is close to the Father's heart, is the one who has made God known (cf. 3:13, 5:37, 6:46, 8:38).

CHAPTER THREE

Act 1: John 1–4
The Messiah Makes
His Debut

CHARACTERIZATIONS OF JESUS

The Lamb of God | Rabbi | Son of Man | Son of God | King of Israel |
Holy Spirit Baptizer | Messiah

SUPPORTING CHARACTERS

Jesus's first disciples | Jesus's mother | Religious leaders | Nicodemus |
The Samaritan woman at the well | The royal official

Scene 1: What's in a Name? (John 1:19–51)

As the last notes of the overture fade, the curtain slowly rises on a
lone figure at the center of the stage. "As Isaiah the prophet said, 'I am
the voice of one crying in the wilderness.'" The man's words reverberate through the theater with authority. "Make straight the way of the
Lord." This is John from the Prologue, who is not the light but witness to the light. John has been baptizing his Jewish siblings—as his
quote from the prophet Isaiah indicates—in preparation for something

ACT 1 PLAYLIST

Scene 1
"Prayer" from *Come From Away*

Scene 2
"Sunrise, Sunset" from *Fiddler on the Roof,*

Scene 3
"The Temple" from *Jesus Christ, Superstar*

Scene 4
"Music of the Night" from *Phantom of the Opera*
"Suddenly, Seymour" from *Little Shop of Horrors*

Scene 5
"Waiting on a Miracle" from *Encanto*

bigger. John moves to the side and gestures behind him to a figure center stage, a man the narrator calls Jesus. John cries out, "Here is the lamb of God who takes away the sins of the world!" Symbols clash in the orchestra.

The statement seems to carry great theological weight but it is vague enough to initiate a ripple of confused whispering through the audience. *What does he mean by the lamb of God? Is he referring to the Passover lamb or a sacrificial lamb or something else? What does it mean to take up the sin of the world?*

John continues, speaking about how he saw the Spirit descend on the man like a dove and how this man is the one who will baptize people in the Holy Spirit. The man center stage has not moved; he does not mime baptism and we do not see a dove. The action John describes seems to have been offstage. The lights dim.

When the lights come back up, John is accompanied by some of his disciples. He gestures again to Jesus and tells his followers to behold the Lamb of God. This initiates a montage of episodes where some disciples seek Jesus and others are sought by him. A jaunty tune plays, the tempo gradually increasing. Over the course of the song, these fledgling disciples reveal much about Jesus's identity by the monikers they call him. Jesus speaks only a few lines, mostly to demonstrate his otherworldly foreknowledge. The words he speaks to Nathanael and the other disciples to end the scene are significant, though: "Very truly, I tell you, you will see heaven opened and the angels of God ascending and descending upon the Son of Man." The song ends on a high, reverberating note.

It will be helpful, I think, for me to provide an interpretive key for this short but significant pericope (or literary unit). John 1:35–51 is the Fourth Gospel's "calling of the disciples" scene but it is notable that the disciples play a very secondary role to Jesus. They serve, in fact, as mouthpieces for a litany of titles that provide John's audience with a quick but profound glimpse at the identity of Jesus. These titles, peppered throughout the brief exchanges the disciples (and John the Baptist) have with Jesus, are worth exploring since the Gospel writer uses them to set a deeply theological tone for the rest of his story about Jesus.

Lamb of God

John the Baptist calls Jesus the *Lamb of God*, who takes up/carries away the sin of the world in both 1:29 and 1:36. This repetitive introduction refers to one aspect of Jesus's salvific mission in John—Jesus taking away the consequences of sin or warding off evil. It is a complicated but pivotal concept to grasp if one wants to understand salvation in John's Gospel. It is also a little mind-blowing because this is rarely talked about in Christian circles. First thing to note is that in John, as opposed to the Synoptics, Jesus dies the day before Passover, on the Day of Preparation when the Passover lamb was killed. This narrative detail points to the likelihood that John's imagery of Jesus as the lamb is not tied to the idea of a sacrificial lamb but to the Passover lamb. The Passover lamb in the exodus story does not atone for Israel's sin; it protects them from death. The blood painted on the doorpost saves them from the force that kills the Egyptian children; death "passes over" the Israelites because of the lamb. This means the function of the lamb's blood is apotropaic—it wards off evil or protects from death.[1]

We also see Jesus's death as apotropaic when Jesus compares himself to the serpent lifted up in the wilderness in John 3:14 (a reference

---

[1] I know this is a lot to handle. If you want to read more about the apotropaic function of the Passover lamb, see Mary Coloe, *John 1–10,* Wisdom Commentary Series (Collegeville, MN: Liturgical Press, 2021), 37–42. See also William Loader, *Jesus in John's Gospel: Structure and Issues in Johannine Christology* (Grand Rapids: Eerdmans, 2017), 162–63.

to Numbers 21:8). The serpent in Numbers, like the Passover lamb's blood, does not atone for the Israelites' complaining disobedience; instead, it wards off death for those who look on it and trust God. When John announces that the *Lamb of God* takes away the sin of the world, the authors could be connecting this image to the Passover Lamb and the serpent, foreshadowing that Jesus will ward off or take away the death that comes from the sin of the world.[2] And let me emphasize that sin here is singular not plural. John does not refer to the individual sins of individual people but to a collective of sin (or one type of sin), which in John's story world is failing to trust that Jesus is the one sent from the Father to show God's character to the world.

Holy Spirit Baptizer

John the Baptist also implies that Jesus is a *Holy Spirit Baptizer* (1:32–34)—that the Holy Spirit came and rested on him so that he might baptize others in the Holy Spirit. In the same breath, John calls Jesus "the Chosen One," which is a title closely related to "Christ/Messiah" (see next title). Jesus's role as the Holy Spirit Baptizer will climax in 20:19–22, when Jesus breathes on the disciples so that the Spirit might empower them.

Rabbi and Messiah

Andrew calls Jesus Rabbi (1:38) and then recognizes him as the *Messiah*, or the *Christ* (meaning anointed one; 1:41). "Rabbi" is a generic but prestigious title for a teacher, but the designation "Messiah" has much more significance and depth for John (the two terms translated as Messiah or Christ are mentioned 19 times in this Gospel). In some

---

[2] Craig R. Koester, *Symbolism in the Fourth Gospel: Community: Meaning, Mystery, Community*, 2nd ed (Minneapolis, MN: Fortress, 2003) 219–24; Sandra Schneiders, "The Lamb of God and the Forgiveness of Sin(s) in the Fourth Gospel," *Catholic Biblical Quarterly* 73 (2011): 16–17.

strands of Jewish thought, the messiah is the anticipated human agent who will accomplish God's restoration of Israel.[3] One example of the first-century idea of messiah appears in Acts 1, when the disciples ask the risen Jesus if he is going to restore the kingdom to Israel (Acts 1:6). In John's Gospel, however, the role of messiah isn't defined in such a narrow—or direct—way. Messiah, for John, is someone who fulfills the witness of John the Baptizer (3:28), reveals truth (at least according to the woman at the well in 4:29), performs signs (10:24–25), and brings resurrection and life (11:25–27). That's about as clear as John makes the role of the messiah in the Gospel. What we do know for sure is that inspiring people to trust Jesus as the Messiah is the central goal of the Johannine authors. Remember John 20:31: "these are written that you may believe (or continue to believe) that Jesus is the Messiah, the Son of God, and that through believing you may have life in his name."

Son of Joseph, Son of God, and King of Israel

From Philip and Nathanael we hear three more designations for Jesus. First, Philip tells Nathanael that Jesus is "him about whom Moses in the Law and also the Prophets wrote, Jesus son of Joseph from Nazareth" (1:45). These descriptions point to Jesus's human origin as the son of Joseph and to his messianic status (something that keeps coming up in this section!). Nathanael doubts that the messiah could come from Nazareth but when he meets Jesus and witnesses a prophetic utterance, he comes around, declaring Jesus to be the "Son of God" and "King of Israel" (1:49). The first

---

[3] The restoration of Israel meant different things to different people during the Second Temple period, that time between the rebuilding of the second Jerusalem Temple around 515 BCE and its later destruction by the Romans in 70 CE. Primarily, the restoration envisioned the scattered Jewish people returning to the land and God freeing them from foreign oppression. This end of oppression would possibly coincide with God's judgment and punishment of the oppressors and be achieved by the rule of a military or spiritual leader known as the messiah.

title highlights a familial connection between God and Jesus, whom John often refers to as the Son of the Father. It also continues a theme from the Prologue, that Jesus has divine origins as well as human ones. However, it is possible that John uses "Son of God" more like the Synoptic Gospels do, to talk about a divinely-chosen leader. This pairs well with Jesus as the "King of Israel," which implies a historical, political function. Jesus, as Son of God and King of Israel, is the ulti-mate Jewish leader guiding Israel into relationship with the Father.[4] The titles "Son of God" and "King of Israel" also connect Jesus—once again—to messianic ideas that are developed in the Hebrew Bible and Second Temple literature.[5]

Son of Man

In 1:51, Jesus calls himself the *Son of Man*, which is a phrase found in the Hebrew Bible, specifically the books of Ezekiel and Daniel. This concluding image is the only self-identification Jesus has made thus far and it works with the disciples' titles to illustrate Jesus's multifaceted mission. The term literally means "human one," but it takes on pro-phetic and apocalyptic significance in the literature of Second Temple Judaism. Depending on the context, the "Son of Man" title has varying connotations. It can refer to a prophet, like Ezekiel, who has divine visions and speaks on behalf of God or to a divine-like figure as in this passage from Daniel 7:13–14:

---

[4] John's Gospel uses the language of Father as a key literary motif. It is import-ant for us to note, however, that the image is a metaphor, as all our language about God is. Although we cannot access the author's original intention in focusing on the father metaphor, it likely has to do with one or all of the fol-lowing: communicating God's parental care, showing Jesus's close, familial relationship to God, and drawing on imagery from the Hebrew Bible that referred to the king as God's son (see Psalm 2 and Psalm 89).
[5] Second Temple literature is a diverse group of texts written in Jewish contexts during the Second Temple period.

As I watched in the night visions,
>   I saw one like a human being [son of man]
>   coming with the clouds of heaven.
>   And he came to the Ancient One
>   and was presented before him.
>   To him was given dominion
>   and glory and kingship,
>   that all peoples, nations, and languages
>   should serve him.
>   His dominion is an everlasting dominion
>   that shall not pass away,
>   and his kingship is one
>   that shall never be destroyed. (NRSVue)

The son of man/human one figure in Daniel 7 is a kingly ruler who comes from the clouds to rule over all peoples in an everlasting kingdom. This is an eschatological vision that becomes the basis for later apocalyptic thought. You may now be wondering, "what's the difference between eschatological and apocalyptic?" I'm glad you asked. Both are complex concepts that are easily misunderstood and yet inescapably relevant to NT backgrounds.

Eschatology is a term that refers to the last things or end times. Jewish thoughts about eschatology varied but the general idea that dominated between the writing of Daniel and Jesus's first-century context was that people were living in an evil age and God would intervene one day to inaugurate the age to come, which would result in judgment against the nations and restoration for Israel.

Apocalyptic thought and literature are connected to eschatology but have their own nuances. An apocalyptic worldview was a way of articulating reality that had become quite popular by the time of Jesus. It envisioned a parallel spiritual realm that corresponded to the earthly realm, full of angels and demons whose activity affected the human experience. In this worldview, God was a transcendent being who was in total control, and revealed truth to humans through divine revelation (often mediated through angels). The apocalyptic *telos*, or end goal for the world, was already predetermined and involved God (and good) winning out over Satan/ the devil (and evil). *Apocalypses*, or apocalyptic literature, reflected this worldview and often arose from groups that were either persecuted or felt persecuted; examples of apocalypses include the second half of Daniel and Revelation.

The "Son of Man" title used in John—which is drawn from Daniel and picked up in the language of Revelation—likely functions in an apocalyptic way, linking Jesus to the climax of history, divine judgment, and God's defeat of evil. This function is not made explicit by the authors of John, but the contextual background certainly leads the reader to assume it. The fact that John combines the title here with the image of Jacob's ladder from Genesis 28 serves at the very least to reiterate Jesus's intermediary role between the divine and human realms and to illustrate his incarnation.

Although the function of this scene (plot-wise) is to show how Jesus gathers disciples for his upcoming mission, the images used here serve a deeper purpose. They provide a big-picture view of who Jesus is and hint at what he will accomplish in the coming acts. The audience learns—just from the montage of monikers announced on stage—that Jesus is a Jewish teacher, the chosen human agent of change/Messiah, the son of the Father, and the true ruler of Israel who will mediate God's presence, communicate God's character, ward off death for humanity, and perhaps inaugurate the climax of history and the defeat of evil in the world. That's quite a lot of roles for one person to fulfill!

Scene 2: Jesus's Coming Out Party (John 2:1–12)

Now that the audience knows, at least vaguely, who Jesus is supposed to be, the Gospel writer starts to reveal more about what Jesus has come to do. He stages a surprise coming out party for Jesus—only it's at someone else's wedding.

At the beginning of the scene, we are introduced to Jesus's mother. I call her "Jesus's mother" because the authors do not give her a name, not in the entire Gospel. Is this because there are too many Marys in the story and they don't want the audience to get confused? Is it because the authors don't know Mary's name? (This is quite possible if John has dependence only on Mark's Gospel; Mark doesn't name Mary either). Is it because the focus of the story is on Jesus's new family, his community of disciples, rather than his earthly family? Or is it perhaps because Mary serves as a representative figure modeling discipleship and belief? It's hard to know for sure (but we can probably rule out the first option).

Weddings are the most joyous of times. Weddings are the most stressful of times. It has probably always been this way because they are by nature liminal spaces, events of transition and transformation for families. Ancient Mediterranean weddings had an additional level of liminality because they were places where the boundaries between men (those of the public space) and women (those of the domestic sphere) were blurred. The society in which Jesus lived was also one in which the concerns for honor and shame ran high. In any public situation, like a wedding, there was potential for a family to add to their honor or detract from it, depending on what happened. The scrabble for honor, and the avoidance of shame, was key to a family's reputation. So how catastrophic do you think it would have been for the family in Cana of Galilee (John 2) that they ran out of wine at their wedding celebration, in front of God and everybody?

Luckily, Jesus's mother was at the wedding, ready to save the honor of the host family (while adding to the honor of her own family as well!). Picture the scene. The music is joyous and loud. Extras are scattered across the stage, chatting and laughing and dancing, all on their way to festive tipsiness. A woman steps forward and starts to sing, "Sunrise, Sunset" (No, wait, that's *Fiddler on the Roof*). You get the picture though. Eventually, the music mutes and a light comes up on Jesus's mother in conversation with her son, who has come to the wedding with some of his disciples. "They have no wine," she tells him. Jesus's answer is not curt or rude but cautious. "Woman, what concern is that to me and to you? My hour has not yet come."

His mother looks unconvinced by his hesitance. So, she turns to the servants of the wedding and tells them to do whatever Jesus tells them to. Before walking off stage, she winks at the audience as if to say, "That's the key: to do what he tells you to do." And she fades into the darkness. A flurry of activity begins. At the command of Jesus, the servants fill six HUGE stone jars—the kind usually meant for purification rites—with water, then draw the water into a goblet to give to the person in charge of the reception.[6]

The steward tastes the water, which is now wine, and walks over to where the groom is. He announces for all to hear, "Everyone serves the good wine first and then the inferior wine after the guests have become drunk. But you have kept the good wine until now." The honor of the family is saved! But, even more importantly, as the narrator then tells us: "Jesus did this, the first of his signs, in Cana of Galilee and revealed his glory, and his disciples believed in him."

My husband and I did not have wine at our wedding. The ceremony and the reception were both held at my home church, a First Baptist Church in central Texas, so not only was wine forbidden but dancing was a no-no too. Our celebratory activity was karaoke, which was fun, but not a festivity everyone participated in. But for the Cana wedding, wine and dancing were central to the celebrations. Jesus may not have been the life of this party, but when he turns 150 gallons of water

---

[6] It is significant that John includes the detail about the water jars being for purification. In this story, instead of using the jars for their ritual purpose, which was probably to purify utensils for the wedding, Jesus uses the jars to initiate a celebration of abundance that looks like the messianic banquet thought to mark the beginning of the new age (see Isaiah 25:6–10, which is quoted in Revelation 21:3–4 in the new heaven and new earth passage). Throughout this Gospel, Jesus is portrayed as offering an alternative form of purification through his presence and ministry.

into wine, he becomes the *source* of the life of the party. And the fact that this life was symbolized by wine is significant: Jewish writings from the time portrayed wine as a sign of the coming age, the libation of the messianic banquet, and even compared the logos—God's word and ordering principle (wink, wink)—to wine. The transformation that Jesus so casually enacts in this wedding scene starts at the *business* end of the Jewish religion—represented by the six stone water jars used for ritual purification—but culminates in a miracle symbolizing the *hopeful* end of their faith. Jesus's first sign is not the healing of a body but the healing of humanity and history. The Messiah has come and is bringing with him new life and a new age.

Scene 3: My Body is a Temple (John 2:13–25)

In the Synoptic Gospels, Jesus's big dramatic scene in the Temple comes near the end of the story. The audience already knows Jesus's character and priorities by then and so when he yells and drives out animals and money changers, it is not overly disturbing. In John's Gospel, the scene happens right after the wedding at Cana, at the very beginning of Jesus's ministry. It's jarring, seeing the man who turned water into wine, whose disciples were just beginning to trust him, throw a temper tantrum in a holy place. Why does John place this scene so early in the narrative and what does it mean? Let's stage it to get some clarity.

Jesus appears from the wings, entering a busy scene complete with people, animals, and commerce. The spotlight follows him. The first thing we see him do is bizarre; he methodically braids together some cords and makes a whip. He then crosses the stage and begins to chase the people and the sacrificial animals off stage. To the dove sellers he commands, "Take these things out of here! Stop making my Father's house a marketplace!" If you have seen the musical *Jesus Christ Superstar*, picture the actor playing Jesus singing impossibly high at the top of his lungs and screaming, "Get out!" This is pure, unadulterated drama. But then the spotlight shifts to the narrator on the far left of the stage and the note cuts short. He explains to the audience: "Jesus's disciples remembered that it was written, 'Zeal for your house will consume me.'" The intensity of the scene dissipates abruptly. The spotlight returns to the scene, where some fellow Jews in the Temple were conversing with Jesus. "What sign can you show us for doing this?"

"Destroy this temple, and in three days I will raise it up."

The Jews scoff, "This temple has been under construction for forty-six years, and will you raise it up in three days?" The narrator's voice interjects with an aside, "But he was speaking of the temple (literally, "sanctuary") of his body." The lights fade and the actors leave the stage. Our narrator leans forward into the spotlight to give the audience a glimpse of the denouement of the story: "After he was raised from the dead, his disciples remembered that he had said this, and they believed the Scripture and the word that Jesus had spoken."

By the end of the scene, it becomes clear that this episode deviates from the Synoptics' accounts, serving a completely different function. In the Synoptics, the temple cleansing is the final straw that motivates Jewish religious authorities to seek Jesus's death (see Mark 11:15–19, Matt 21:12–17; Luke 19:45–48). Here, the scene is like a first straw, setting up tension and focusing not on the offenses of the merchants or the anger of the Jewish authorities but on Jesus's identity and purpose. We can see this in the quote John introduces here, from Psalm 69:9—"Zeal for your house will consume me."[7] What could

---

[7] Important interpretive lesson: When the New Testament authors quote or allude to Hebrew Bible passages, readers need to take note. They usually include verses or images in order to make connections with their audience, to tie together themes or to give clues about deeper meaning in their writing. Scholars have noted that the way New Testament authors interpret the Hebrew Bible sometimes shows flexibility of interpretation or even disregard for the original context. With that said, we need to pay attention to what connections New Testament writers are making, but we should not project their interpretations back onto the original writings. When John quotes from Psalm 69 here, he is not saying that the psalmist was thinking about Jesus or prophesying this event; instead, John wants to forge a link between Jesus and his actions and the history of the temple in Israel.

have been a wildly chaotic scene focused on the sins of the authorities becomes a vehicle to say more about Jesus and his disciples. John wants the audience to know that Jesus's body is the true temple; it is the place where heaven and earth converge, where God's presence dwells among the people. The narrator's comments fast-forward in time and antici-pate the climax of the story—Jesus's body will also die and be raised from the dead. So, stay tuned, John seems to say to his audience. You wouldn't want to miss that.

Scene 4: Nicodemus at Night vs. the Samaritan Bride (John 3–4:42)

The next two stories in John are linked. If we imagined it on stage, the first part of the scene, Jesus's conversation with Nicodemus, would happen farther back from the audience, set upstage right. The second part of the scene, Jesus's conversation with a woman at a well, would occur upstage and on the opposite side from the Nicodemus vignette. Although the stories are separate in John, an ambitious director might overlap the two conversations, switching back and forth to highlight the contrasts.

The lighting on Jesus and Nicodemus is low; the important Jewish leader comes to Jesus under the cover of night, after all. There is a clan-destine feel to the conversation. When the focus shifts stage left, to the Samaritan woman, the lighting is bright, almost harsh. Jesus has stopped at Jacob's well at midday and interacts with the woman in broad daylight.

What ties these two episodes together is that Jesus reveals important details about his identity and his mission in both conversations; they, in turn, both question him and misunderstand him at various points in the conversation. That is where the similarities end. While the Jewish insider persists in missing the point and eventually stops participating in the conversation, the Samaritan outsider (who is equal parts polit-ical enemy, religious misfit, and social reject in relationship to Jesus) engages deeply with the mysterious man who asks her for a drink. She holds her own against Jesus and after he reveals the truth that he has not shared with anyone—he is the Messiah!—the woman takes that truth to the people of her village and becomes the first evangelist in John's Gospel.

Jesus's dialogue with Nicodemus (3:1–21) is full of contrasting images. This Johannine dualism, common in writings that take an apocalyptic worldview, uses exaggerated opposites to persuade the audience to trust in Jesus. The divergent images of heaven and earth are the guiding symbols here—Jesus tells Nicodemus that to see the kingdom of God he must be born from above (or "again," both meanings could be in view here, a double entendre), that if he doesn't understand earthly things he cannot understand heavenly, and that only the Son of Man ascended and descended from heaven.[8]

Jesus also speaks of flesh and spirit, extending the metaphor to introduce an important character, the Spirit (3:4–10). Entry into the kingdom, or salvation as we call it today, requires a Spirit birth into a new family in addition to a creaturely or fleshly birth. The Spirit will become more important in later dialogues but her presence here serves to explain how followers of Jesus attain the deeper level of understanding required for trust in God.[9]

The next part of the scene (3:16–21) makes use of two sets of contrasting images: those who believe/trust (represented metaphorically as those who come to the light and those who have eternal life) and those who do not believe/trust (represented metaphorically by those who love darkness rather than light and by those who perish). The word

---

[8] Scholar Benjamin Reynolds understands John as an "apocalyptic gospel," with Jesus as not just a human mediator who *receives* revelation from God, which is common in apocalypses, but as the *revelation itself* as well ("Rethinking the Jewish Apocalypses: Rethinking the Genre of John's Gospel," in *John's Gospel and Intimations of Apocalyptic*, ed. Catrin H. Williams and Christopher Rowland [London: Bloomsbury, 2013], 54–56).

[9] I use the pronoun "she" for the Holy Spirit here to balance out the exclusively masculine language for God that has dominated Church history.

that we translate as "believe" (*pistis* or *pisteuo*) also means "to put faith in/to trust in." When John uses the word, it carries the connotation of action (to follow); it is not merely an academic or mental exercise. In my Protestant evangelical context, the meaning of "believe" has deteriorated, coming to signify assent to a set of beliefs without action attached to it. Since this is a shadow of the original meaning, I will try to use "trust" more than "believe" when this word appears. It makes a difference:

> For God loved the world in this way, that God gave the one and only son, so that everyone who trusts (and follows) Jesus will not perish but will have eternal life (John 3:16, my translation).

Salvation comes to those who trust in who Jesus is and follow him, the one who is the light. This salvation can be observed in the present because those who follow him come to the light and possess a quality of life known as "eternal life." Those who do not trust Jesus have condemned themselves; you can tell who they are because their deeds are evil and they avoid the light.

A brief note on John's use of the words "life" and "eternal life," as he uses them far more frequently than the Synoptics do, and does so in surprising ways: I know we think of eternal life as "after we die" life, but John does not limit this life to later—it starts in the now. For John, eternal life begins after one has been "born from above" (3:3) to become a child of God (1:12–13) and he often portrays a follower of Jesus as having eternal life in the present (3:15–16; 6:47, 6:54, 6:68). Though he does not ignore the future implications of eternal life completely (6:39–40; 12:48), the emphasis is predominantly on God's present saving activity. Closely related to the idea of eternal life in the present is what later theologians call "realized eschatology" (or inaugurated eschatology), a theory that locates the end times in the life, death, and resurrection of Jesus, not in a future time. Inaugurated eschatology teaches that the age to come (Jewish terminology) or the kingdom of God (Synoptic Gospels terminology) or eternal life (John's language) has already arrived with Jesus's ministry. A key example of what might be called inaugurated eschatology comes in John 5:24–25:

> "Very truly, I tell you, anyone who hears my word and believes him who sent me *has eternal life* and does not come under judgment but has passed from death to life. Very truly, I tell you, the hour is coming and *is now here* when the dead will hear the voice of the Son of God, and those who hear will live (NRSVue, emphasis mine).

The scene with Nicodemus presents a panoply of mixed metaphors but it does so because who Jesus is and how he brings salvation is complex. In addition to learning that salvation requires a spiritual birth into a new family and is marked by a new quality of life forged in the light, we learn that the light, Jesus, has to be lifted up to make eternal life available to the world. This reference to a bizarre story from Numbers 21 may be one of the clearest expressions of what John thinks is happening on the cross. And it's about as clear as mud. In the Numbers scene, fiery serpents have been let loose in the camp of Israel as punishment for their grumbling and unfaithfulness; the serpents bite them and many die. Desperate, the people repent of their actions, so God commands Moses to raise up a bronze serpent for the people to look at. When they gaze upon the lifted serpent, they live.

John seems to be communicating that people receive life (eternal life) when they look at (put trust in) Jesus who will be lifted up on the cross. To heal the world from the serpents' bites (maybe a reference to the evil forces in the world), Jesus will be lifted up for all to see. Why must this be the case? What exactly happens on the cross to give life to the world? It is hard to decipher. But this much we know from

Jesus's conversation with Nicodemus: Jesus is the one who offers life and it involves him losing his own.[10]

In the story of the Samaritan woman at the well (4:1–42), we find the longest conversation Jesus has with anyone in the Gospels. It is astonishing that the dialogue happens between a man and a woman—such conversations would only occur between spouses or family members—but the real shocker is that the woman is a Samaritan. For centuries, Samaritans and Jews occupied neighboring lands and practiced similar religions while actively expressing feelings of animosity toward one another. The origin of the Samaritan people remains a mystery, but ancient Jewish explanations of Samaritan origins were overwhelmingly negative. The prevailing Jewish explanation of Jesus's time associates the Samaritans with the Cutheans, descendants of the colonists referred to in 2 Kings 17:24–41. Supposedly, when the northern tribes of Israel were led into captivity by the Assyrians, settlers were sent from Cutha (near Babylon) to populate Samaria, the area where the Israelites had lived. These peoples then adapted Israelite religion into their own practices and formed a faith that eventually revolved around the Torah and their own temple. Other Jewish sources suggest that the Samaritan people originated with the priests and other Israelites who either fled or were exiled from their people when they refused to send their foreign wives away during the resettlement of Jerusalem

---

[10] I have omitted from this theatrical version of John a scene that the authors place between the stories of Nicodemus and the woman at the well: John 3:22–36 (which may function as an extended ending to the Nicodemus scene). The passage focuses briefly on John the Baptist and how both he and Jesus were baptizing people in Judea. John's disciples express concern that so many are flocking to Jesus but John calms their fears by downplaying his role (e.g., I am not the Messiah, I am only the friend of the bridegroom, I must decrease and he must increase). The conclusion of this section reads like a condensed version of the Gospel's claims about Jesus: Jesus is the one sent from God and so his testimony is true and offers life. I cut the scene because it seems to be one that is addressed to the Gospel's first audience, which perhaps included followers of John the Baptist. We, today, are in no danger of exalting John over Jesus so I didn't think we needed the scene here.

post-Babylonian exile (see Ezra 10). Archaeological evidence suggests the Samaritans remained at least as monotheistic as Israelites, whatever their origins, so the negative appraisals of Samaritans we find in our Bible do not take into account the full picture. They should have been more like Israel's siblings than enemies, but that is not the story history tells. The Jewish–Samaritan enmity climaxed in 128 BCE when John Hyrcanus, high priest and Hasmonean ruler of the Jews, conquered the Samaritan capital city of Shechem and later destroyed the Samaritan temple on Mount Gerazim. It is not surprising, then, that these groups remained bitter enemies at least until the first century CE.

What is surprising, though, is that Jesus would cut through Samaria while fleeing the religious forces that were hostile to him in Judea. He stops at a well in the heat of the day and asks a woman for water. After she responds with incredulity that he would want a drink from her, Jesus proceeds to speak about the living water she could receive from him. The woman's reply, "Are you greater than our ancestor Jacob, who gave us the well?" focuses on the common ground of the Israelite history they share. With this shared foundation, Jesus engages her in a revealing conversation about water, himself, and the worship of God.

Jesus compares the water he offers her to springs of living water, like the kind found in rivers and sometimes used for baptism. Water is an important symbol for new life (or eternal life) in the Gospel of John. We've already seen John baptizing, Jesus turning water into the best wine, and Jesus encouraging his followers to be born of water and spirit in the Nicodemus dialogue. The woman asks for this water (and the new life?) but then the story takes a sharp turn: "Go, call your husband, and come back," Jesus says to her.

Why does Jesus seem to change the subject here? Well, it has to do with the well. In Genesis 29, Jacob meets his future wife, Rachel, at a well at midday. A generation before, Abraham's servant had found Isaac's wife, Rebekah, at a well (Gen 24). Biblical scholar Robert Alter labels repeated settings like these "biblical type-scenes" and he calls the meeting-at-a-well trope a betrothal type-scene.[11] The first Christians to experience John's Gospel read aloud would have recognized this type-scene as soon as they heard that Jesus stopped at a well at noon.

And with Jesus's mention of husbands, John finally gives the audience what they've been expecting—a reference to marriage. What they did not expect, though, was that the woman in the scene was not a blushing bride-to-be but a wedding-weary woman. Preachers love to play up the scandal of the woman's multiple husbands, characterizing the Samaritan as a serial divorcée or an unfaithful tramp. But these interpretations stray from the actual text, injecting modern sensibilities (and misogynistic assumptions) into the story. Neither Jesus nor the Gospel writers make a value statement about the five husbands; it is likely the woman's past is not her fault. As a woman, she could not initiate divorce; she could have also been widowed and remarried multiple times.

So, if Jesus is not shaming the woman, why does he mention marriage? Many commentators interpret the woman's husbands symbolically, as representative of either the five political powers that had ruled Samaria or the five groups that were rumored to have comprised the early Samaritan people. In this view, Jesus is rehearsing Samaritan history. Perhaps this betrothal type–scene doesn't anticipate the marriage of a couple but of the Samaritans and their God (or the Samaritans and the Jews!). Jesus tells the woman that soon all people will worship not divided but together in Spirit and truth. Jesus then gives the Samaritan woman insight into the mysterious nature of God—God is Spirit!—and invites her into the reality of this divine truth.

If this conversation were a musical number, the climax of the song would start with the following line, a wistful insight from the Samaritan: "I know that Messiah is coming and when he comes, he will proclaim

---

[11] Robert Alter, *The Art of Biblical Narrative* (New York: Basic books, 1981), 51–52.

all things to us" (John 4:25). The Samaritans, like the Jews, anticipated the arrival of an eschatological messianic figure, called the *Taheb*. The *Memar Marqah*, a Samaritan document from the third century BCE, says, "The *Taheb* will come and reveal the truth." It makes sense, then, that Jesus's disclosure of the Samaritan's truth prompted her hopeful comment about the Messiah. The climax would peak with Jesus's vulnerable line of self-disclosure: "I am (he) … the one speaking to you" (4:26).

This is the first "I am" statement in John. The Johannine "I am" statements come in two forms: affirmations in which Jesus simply replies, "I am," and statements like, "I am the bread of life." Here, Jesus says only "I am," but in the context, he means, "I am the Messiah." This is the central truth of the Gospel of John (see 20:30–31) and it is the only time that Jesus reveals this truth to another person. That the person he trusts himself to is a Samaritan *and* a woman is deeply significant, not only to John's first-century audience but also to anyone who seeks to understand the Gospel. The truth of Jesus's life is that he brings a new way of life, a way that results in all people—women and men, Samaritans and Jews, religious outsiders and religious insiders—worshiping in Spirit and in truth.

At the scene's end, the woman runs off stage, eager to tell the people of her Samaritan village about Jesus, the Messiah and revealer of truth. While the dialogue between Nicodemus and Jesus concluded with the religious leader's confusion and indecision, the conversation at the well with the outsider woman results in her and her people becoming followers of Jesus.[12] Her positive response to the truth Jesus

---

[12] Colleen M. Conway analyzes John's portrayal of five female characters and five male characters and concludes women are presented positively in John's narrative while the men are presented inconsistently. For example, Nicodemus, Pilate, and Peter are characterized in negative ways, while the man healed from blindness and the Beloved Disciple have positive characterizations. See *Men and Women in the Fourth Gospel: Gender and Johannine Characterization*, Society of Biblical Literature Dissertation Series 167 (Atlanta: Society of Biblical Literature, 1999).

shares becomes the model response to Jesus; she trusts Jesus and acts on that faith to become the first (and, arguably, the most effective) evangelist of John's Gospel.

Scene 5: Only Trust Him (John 4:46–54)

The final scene in Act 1 feels brief compared to the extended scenes with Nicodemus and the Samaritan evangelist. It provides a fitting conclusion, though, to these series of scenes that reveal Jesus's supernatural signs and otherworldly wisdom; scenes in which the witnesses respond with either trust or ambivalence. Here, the lights come up on Jesus and a man who kneels before him in a posture of pleading. The man's son is dying and he begs Jesus to heal him. Jesus sighs, "Unless you see signs and wonders, you will not put your trust in me" (4:48). But the man is a royal official and he has shown enough faith to shame himself, groveling publicly at the feet of a traveling preacher. So, Jesus tells him to go, assuring him the son would live. The royal official follows Jesus's instructions. He jumps up to rush home and in doing so, he displays faith in Jesus and his words. And, of course, he has placed his trust in the right place. The son is healed, an act that takes place off stage.

It might seem odd to those familiar with the Synoptic Gospels that Jesus performs this healing act so late in the narrative and in such a brief, inconspicuous passage. In contrast, Mark's Gospel presents healing miracles almost immediately after Jesus's baptism and in rapid succession: Mark 1:21–45 tells of Jesus performing an exorcism, healing Peter's mother-in-law, cleansing a man with a skin disease, and basically going on a healing tour. Jesus's healing actions in the Synoptics serve to announce and exemplify the nature of God's kingdom and to show Jesus's powers over the forces of sickness, evil, and death in the world. In John, however, healing miracles function differently. Jesus's first healing comes after Jesus's power, importance, and connection to God have already been established in the Prologue, through the titles the disciples give him, with his messianic miracle at the wedding, and in his conversations with Nicodemus and the Samaritan woman. The healing of the official's son does not add much to John's portrait of Jesus, but it does establish the inferior role that healing miracles play in the story. Jesus's healing action here is almost a concession; he seems to lament that people desire signs and wonders for faith. The miracle results in an entire household coming to trust Jesus—and this response of belief is the goal of the whole narrative. In the next act, though, we will see that Jesus's next healing miracle results not in belief but in opposition and controversy. Healing, at least in John, is not the sign of the kingdom that it is in the Synoptic Gospels. It is just one way among many that people begin to follow Jesus the Messiah.

And so, with the royal official's disappearance from the stage, the curtain descends on Act 1 and the narrator appears at the front of the stage to deliver his closing line. "So he himself trusted, along with his whole household" (4:53). With these words, the audience comes to understand that there has been a refrain running through these scenes, one that is leading them on a journey that will continue through the coming acts. It is a refrain that sounds like a song we used to sing in Baptist churches, "Only trust Him, only trust Him, only trust Him now; He will save you, He will save you, He will save you now." When Jesus brought life to the party and turned water into wine, his disciples trusted him. When he cleared the Jerusalem temple, the religious authorities balked but others believed in him because of it. Jesus revealed truth to a religious insider and an enemy outsider; Nicodemus could not bring himself to trust but the Samaritan woman came to such a hopeful faith that she shared the news with her people. Finally, a royal official, whose pride and position should have prevented him from trusting, nevertheless places his faith in Jesus to heal his son. Act 1 concludes with a question hanging in the air, the chorus to a song the actors have been singing in every scene: "Will you trust in Jesus as we have? He's everything we didn't even know we needed…"

CHAPTER FOUR

Act 2: John 5–8 Jesus: Love Him or Leave Him

CHARACTERIZATIONS OF JESUS

The Son of the Father | The Son of Man who will judge the world |
The prophet (who is to come into the world) | The Bread of Life |
The Light of the World

SUPPORTING CHARACTERS

Religious leaders | The man healed by the pool | Jesus's family members |
The crowds | The disciples who stay and the disciples who go

Scene 1: Can I Get a Witness? (John 5)

Everyone loves a good courtroom scene. Whether it's Gregory Peck as
Atticus Finch captivating the jury with his gravelly voice of reason (*To
Kill a Mockingbird*), Billy Flynn and Roxie Hart giving the jury the
old "Razzle Dazzle" (*Chicago*), or Jack Nicholson screaming, "You can't
handle the truth!" (*A Few Good Men*), the drama of the courtroom
never disappoints. In the Gospels, Jesus participates in several different

trials and most of them come at the end of the story, when Jesus is on trial for his life. In John, though, we find a scene near the start of Jesus's ministry when he is on trial for his identity. This placement continues John's narratively early escalation of tension between Jesus and religious authorities (which started with John's comparatively early positioning of the temple clearing up). The trial doesn't take place in a courtroom, but Jesus does defend himself according to the rules of ancient rhetoric and so the audience realizes that John has purposely set the scene up *like* a trial.[1] John wants to communicate with artistic flair that what Jesus reveals about himself on the witness stand carries great weight in this story.

The scene starts with Jesus going to Jerusalem again for a festival. If you are keeping track, Jesus has already been to Jerusalem at least once for a festival, when he clears the temple at Passover time. In John, Jesus takes frequent trips into Jerusalem, whereas the Synoptic Gospels only have Jesus going to Jerusalem during his last week, the week he is crucified. These differences (some might say contradictions!) regarding Jesus's travel have caused much consternation for interpreters. John's Gospel mentions three Passovers, which leads us to believe Jesus's public ministry lasted three years. The Synoptics include only one Passover in their narratives—Jesus's Last Supper with the disciples—and that

---

[1] Several Johannine scholars comment on the rhetorical features of this episode. Kasper Bro Larsen classifies this healing story as a *recognition parody*, crafted in the style of ancient rhetorical dramas which made use of recognition and reversal. The man by the pool should have realized and acknowledged who Jesus was after the healing miracle, but the fact that he does not introduces ambiguity into the story and perhaps catches the audience, who would expect recognition, off guard (*Recognizing the Stranger: Recognition Scenes in the Gospel of John* [Leiden: Brill, 2008], 145–7). Jo-Ann A. Brant suggests the story follows the pattern of persuasive speech found in ancient rhetorical handbooks and the healing part of the episode serves as the *narratio*, which is the first element of a speech that introduces the statement of the case against someone. The accusation stated against Jesus is that he violated the Sabbath, something he will also be accused of in the parallel story of the healing of the man born with blindness in John 9. See Brant's commentary, *John* (Grand Rapids, MI: Baker Academic, 2011), 97–9.

may imply a one-year ministry. So, which is it? Was Jesus's ministry one year or three? The Church today prefers John's assumed timeline, although it is probably not wise to conclude the three Passovers in the story point to a definitive three-year ministry. For all the Gospel writers, historical details like chronology and timelines are secondary concerns to narrative themes and storytelling. The Synoptics don't seem preoccupied with telling us

~~~~~~~~~~~~~~~~~~~~

ACT 2 PLAYLIST

Scene 1
"Razzle Dazzle" from *Chicago*

Scene 2
"Born to Hand Jive" from *Grease,*
"Take Me or Leave Me" from *Rent,*
"Eat Me" by Ozzy Osbourne

Scene 3
"One Jump Ahead" from *Aladdin,*
"Cabinet Battle #1" from *Hamilton*

~~~~~~~~~~~~~~~~~~~~

how long Jesus's public ministry lasted; it clearly wasn't important to them. John doesn't make it explicit either, and although there is a focus on Jesus attending festivals, we cannot assume that John's purpose in recounting these is historicity.

What we can assume is that Jewish religious institutions, like the festivals, are an important theme in John's Gospel. The authors use them to provide a framework for the healing and teaching Jesus does. In Act One, Jesus performs a miraculous sign using the water from jars meant for religious purification; the wine miracle begins the messianic banquet and introduces a new way people can experience God (in addition to the purification system). Then, during Passover, Jesus claims his body is the temple—the place of God's presence—at the very time the Jewish people were celebrating God's rescuing presence with them during the exodus.

Here, Jesus heals a man on the Sabbath, performing God's work on God's day, and the setting of a festival intensifies the transformative (and transgressive) nature of Jesus's miraculous work. He sends a challenging message to religious leaders who preside over holy festivals: "You may claim to celebrate the divine character and God's work among the people, but when Jesus shows you God's character by compassionately healing people, you refuse to recognize it."

It makes for a dramatic scene. The lights come up on a frail man sitting on a mat on the ground, far stage right. The narrator introduces him as a man who has not walked for thirty-eight years, who perches by a pool they call Beth-zatha (or Bethesda). He is waiting for someone to help him into the waters of the pool, which he believes can heal him. Jesus enters from stage left, descending stairs that take him into the pool area. He crosses the stage and we hold our breath, anticipating what will happen next. Jesus reaches the man and asks bluntly, "Do you want to be made well?" The man laments that he has no one to put him into the pool. Jesus doesn't even glance at the so-called healing waters as he commands, "Stand up, take your mat and walk."

The man does just that and it is obvious that he never needed the waters from the pool; he only needed Jesus's authoritative voice calling him to life and wholeness. The narrator's voice then interrupts the scene to provide a vital plot point, "Now that day was a Sabbath." Gasps can be heard from the audience. They know that picking up a mat and carrying it constituted work according to Jewish law and practice, and Jesus not only condoned this, but commanded it.[2]

A spotlight focuses on a group of formal-looking men gathered in front of the stairs. As the newly healed man strolls by the group of Jewish leaders, mat in hand, they are quick to jump on his flagrant flouting of the law. The leaders question him sternly and eventually the man rats Jesus out. They then turn their attention to Jesus, crossing the stage to accuse him of working on the Sabbath. Jesus says only one thing in response: "My Father is still working, and I also am working." It is the wrong thing to say. Jesus's disregard for the Sabbath, combined with his claim to be equal with the Father, make the Jewish leaders see red. They gather in a huddle and we can hear them plotting harm, even death, for Jesus the Sabbath healer.

---

[2] Although the Hebrew Bible does not provide an exhaustive list of activities prohibited on the Sabbath, Jeremiah 17:21–22 does explicitly forbid carrying things and Jewish customs in the first century generally adhered to this prohibition.

Jesus slowly walks up the stairs, stopping just high enough that everyone can see him. He clears his throat to get the attention of the room, then launches into what amounts to an opening statement. Jesus lays out several points: 1) whatever the Father does, he, the Son, does also; 2) the Father has sent him to give life; and 3) he is the Son of Man who will raise the dead at the end of age and judge the world. This last claim draws on the apocalyptic imagery we have already talked about from Daniel. Jesus is basically saying, "You want to plot my death? Go ahead. I am the one who has power over death, who will oversee the judgment of all humanity. There is much more at stake than you think."

Then Jesus calls his witnesses to back up these audacious claims. First up is John the Baptist. "Remember how impressed you were by his message?" Jesus says to the Jewish leaders (and audience). "Well, he testifies on my behalf." And that's not all. Jesus tells them that the God they worship but don't really know at all testifies on his behalf. If they knew the voice of the Father, they would know the voice of the Son.

Jesus's third witness is the Scriptures: "The Scriptures you love so much testify about me." Jesus is on a roll now, "If you knew them, you would know to come to me for life; as it is, you don't understand or have the love of God in you." Then Jesus gives his parting shot, turning the table on the religious leaders: "Moses wrote about me too and he would be ashamed of how little you understand. If you trusted him, you would trust me. But you don't. So, Moses will accuse you even as you stand there accusing me." Jesus turns from them and ascends the stairs, disappearing from view.

On stage, the Jewish leaders storm off in a huff, rejecting Jesus's message just as he said they would. In the audience, though, whispers of recognition start to spread. He claimed to be the Messiah in the scene with the Samaritan woman. Now he calls himself the Son of the Father and the Son of Man, defending himself with John the Baptist, the Scriptures, Moses, and God. If this man is who he claims to be, it would be a game changer. Should we trust his words, his signs, his authority? Or consider him a threat like the religious leaders believed him to be? The jury is still out...

Scene 2: Bread! The Big Dance Number (John 6)

Although the religious leaders continue to reject Jesus and his audacious claims, there are crowds of people who see his signs and follow him. They want more of his miraculous displays. One particular day as Passover is drawing near (again, the religious festival motif!), Jesus goes up a mountain in Galilee and sits down to survey the crowds who have come to him. Thousands clamor for him and as they gather, they take on the appearance of a flash mob. On stage, the scene would be teeming with extras and there would be a kinetic energy building throughout the theater.

Not yet overwhelmed by their fickle attention, Jesus decides to feed the mob. He questions his disciples, "Where are we to buy bread for these people to eat?" It is a trick question. His disciples witnessed the miracle of the water to wine so perhaps they will have faith in Jesus's power. If Jesus could get people drunk on vast quantities of water, surely he could feed them. Philip doesn't catch on, complaining about the cost of feeding so many but Andrew, Simon Peter's brother, tentatively suggests a solution: "A boy has five barley loaves and two fish," he offers. Then doubt creeps in, "But what are they among so many people?"

It is enough for Jesus. So, they sit 5,000-plus people down, feed them and there is an abundance left over—twelve baskets. If the disciples hadn't already caught on at the Cana wedding, surely this miracle would call to their minds the passage about the day of the Lord, the beginning of the new age:

> The threshing floors shall be full of grain;
>> The vats shall overflow with the wine and oil...
> You shall eat in plenty and be satisfied
>> and praise the name of the LORD your God,
>> who has dealt wondrously with you.
> And my people shall never again be put to shame.
> You shall know that I am in the midst of Israel

and that I, the LORD, am your God and there is no other.
And my people shall never again be put to shame.

(Joel 2:24, 26–27, NRSVue)

The abundance of food that satisfies the crowd should be a sign for
them that God is in their midst. But that is a hard concept for even
those closest to Jesus to understand. They settle instead on something
easier to accept: "This is indeed the Prophet who is to come into the
world." A prophet isn't God but it's exciting enough to cause a stir. In
their excitement, the crowd rises like a cresting wave, surging forward,
intent on taking Jesus by force and making him king. Jesus steps off to
the side and fades in the shadows, withdrawing from the mob.

The scene shifts to the next day, after the disciples had crossed
the sea by boat (and had witnessed Jesus walking on water).[3] The disciples, Jesus, and the curious crowds have reconvened. The stage is packed
with people wanting more of what they got the day before. What
happens next plays out like a musical dance number on stage, a call
and response between the masses and Jesus:

The crowd: "Bread! Bread! Give us more bread." *They chant
and jazz run across the stage, intent on swarming Jesus. The orchestra*

---

[3] You may be saying, "Wait, wait! Why did you skip over the walking on water
incident?" Don't fret! I have a good reason. This brief narrative feels like
an awkward intrusion in the middle of the larger story of Jesus giving bread
and Jesus being the bread. It's possible the authors inserted it here because they
were familiar either with the oral tradition behind Mark or with Mark itself,
because the water walking comes right after the feeding of the 5,000 in Mark
6:45–52. Here, the account is abbreviated and does not advance the plot
or theme much. The only purpose it might serve is to add to the evidence
of Jesus's divine status (crossing bodies of water is a way ancient literature
hinted at divine powers—see Brant, *John*, 118) or to show the disciples' fear
and misunderstanding of Jesus. The episodes end differently, too. In Mark,
Jesus gets in the boat after the disciples see him, but in John "they wanted
to take him into the boat, and immediately the boat reached the land toward
which they were going" (6:52). This implies an uncontrollability (maybe unpre-
dictability) to Jesus, which we will see more of in the bread of life discourse.

starts to play a song with a fast, almost frantic, rock beat (think "Born to Hand Jive" from Grease).

Jesus: "You've come to me for food that perishes but the Son of Man can give you food for eternal life." *Jesus whirls away from them, remaining out of their reach to wait for their response.*

The crowd: "What must we do? What must we do?" *They stop just short of Jesus and jump up and down, flinging their hands up in unison.*

Jesus: "Trust in the one God has sent." *Jesus gestures to himself so it is clear who he means.*

The crowd: "What sign will you give for us to trust? Moses gave our ancestors manna in the desert—can you give us some?" *They reach toward him as one, greedy hands grabbing, and then look up, waiting for bread to fall from the heavens.*

Jesus: "It was God who gave, not Moses, and now God gives you the true bread from heaven, the life for the world." *He backs up one step and bows with a flourish, looking to a modern audience like a circus master presiding over the center ring.*

The crowd: "Give us this bread always." *They begin to pirouette, spinning to the beat.* "Always." *They spin faster.* "Always." *The tempo increases and their turns become manic.* "Always." *Finally, they fall to the ground in exhaustion and the music stops. The stage goes dark.*

Jesus: *A spotlight shines on Jesus and his next words puncture the silence with staccato force—*"I. am. the. Bread. of. Life." *Jesus starts to sing acapella, beckoning to the audience with his tenor voice.* "Whoever comes to me will never be hungry, and whoever believes in me will never be thirsty." *The lights come up on the crowd and they remain prone, staring up at him with startled looks. Jesus turns to face* *them.* "But you have seen me and do not trust me. I have come down from heaven not to do my own will but the will of God who sent me." *Jesus turns back to the audience.* "This is the will of my Father, that all who see the Son and trust him may have a different kind of life, and I will raise them up on the last day."

The crowds: "What is he saying now? That he has come down from heaven?" *Slowly, the crowds rise and start to grumble amongst themselves. But Jesus's solo is not over yet. The music starts up again, more ballad than rock.*

Jesus: "No one can come to me unless drawn by the Father who sent me, and I will raise that person up on the last day. Everyone who has heard and learned from the Father comes to me and trusts in me. Your ancestors may have eaten manna in the wilderness, but they died. Whoever eats of this bread will live forever; the bread that I will give for the life of the world is my flesh."

The crowd: "Give us his flesh to eat? His flesh?" *They echo the words with disgust, spitting them out over and over again as they creep backwards away from Jesus.*

Jesus: "I said what I said." *The spotlight on Jesus turns red, bathing him in a blood-tinged light.* "Unless you chomp down on the flesh of the Son of Man and drink his blood, you have no life in you. My flesh is true food, and my blood is true drink." *The music from the pit screeches as it cuts off mid-note. Most of the crowd has backed away and one by one they now disappear, some escaping backstage, others hurrying down the stairs, up the aisles, and out the doors. The audience can catch bits and pieces of their protests as they go.*

The crowd: "Absurd…I'm no cannibal…he sounds like a pagan… this is too much…I'm out."

Jesus: "Does this offend you?" *The dance number has come to an awkward halt and Jesus directs his attention to the only people left on stage, a large group of disciples.* "I told you that no one can come to me unless it is granted by the Father." *His words aren't enough. More disciples turn from him and walk away, shaking their heads. Jesus looks at the twelve with a sad smile.* "Do you also wish to go away?"

Simon Peter: "Lord, to whom can we go? You have the words of life. We trust and know that you are the Holy One of God." *Jesus and the disciples hold their position on stage as the lights sputter out.*

This is the most bizarre scene in John's Gospel—and that is saying a lot. It starts out harmlessly, very much like the Synoptics' accounts of the feeding of the five thousand (fun fact: this is the only miracle that occurs in all four Gospels). John takes the imagery and the weirdness much further, though. Only in John does the feeding occur at Passover and that sets the scene for a connection to Moses (as well as plays into the Jewish festivals motif!). It is only natural, then, that the crowds call him a prophet and then, the next day, asks him for manna from heaven. But Jesus's reply stuns them: You want manna, you got manna. (It's me. Hi. I'm the manna, it's me.) When Jesus tells the crowds, "I am the bread of life," he draws their attention back to the feeding miracle and makes the first of seven "I am" statements found in John's Gospel. These seven "I am" statements contain descriptions ("I am the bread of life") and replies that echo Jesus's answer to the woman at the well (simply, "I am"). While the "I am" statements are literary devices, they also make theological claims. The words *"ego eimi"* are the Greek translation of the self-identifier God used with Moses in Exodus 3: "I am." Although the connection may seem subtle to English-speakers in the 21st century, this wordplay would have been obvious to the first audience of John's Gospel, who would have easily understood the rhetorical identification of Jesus with God.

Next, things turn eucharistic—at least that's what many scholars think. By eucharistic I mean Jesus sounds here like he does in the Synoptic Gospels' Last Supper scenes. In those, Jesus takes the bread and breaks it, giving it to the disciples. In Luke 22:19–20, he says, "This is my body, which is given for you. Do this in remembrance of me." He then takes the cup and says, "This cup that is poured out for you is the new covenant in my blood" (see also Mark 14:22–24, Matthew 26:26–28). But in John's Last Supper scene (John 13), there is no broken bread or poured out wine. It isn't even a Passover meal! And so this chapter—with the feeding sign and Jesus's peculiar speech to the masses—feels like John's nod to the Lord's Supper, complete with sacrificial meal elements. In 6:51, Jesus declares: "Whoever eats of this bread will live forever, and the bread that I will give for the life of the world is my flesh." The elements of the Synoptics' Last Supper are here—bread and body (or flesh) with a salvific aim—but with the twist of John's "life" and "world" language.

Here, though, unlike in the Last Supper scenes, the cannibalistic language is taken to the next level. The second time Jesus talks about his flesh (6:53), he uses the word *esthiō*, which does not just mean "eat"—it's better translated as "chomp" or "munch." It sounds like something out of a zombie flick: "Very truly, I tell you, unless you munch on the flesh of the Son of Man and drink his blood, you have no life in you." Okay, not just zombies but zombies AND vampires. *The Walking Dead* meets *Twilight*. By utilizing this language, Jesus's speech moves from persuasive to offensive, effectively upping the ante for people who want to follow him.[4] No wonder John tells us that many in the crowd stopped following Jesus: this was more than they signed up for. They came seeking signs and wonders, but to witness the true miracle—the identity of Jesus—they had to push through Jesus's cryptic claims and trust that following him was worth the weird. Eventually, the audience will have to decide that as well.

---

[4] Brant, *John*, 124.

Scene 3: The Great Debate (John 7–8)

When the next scene starts, time has passed, and we know this because Jesus is at yet another festival—the fall holiday called *Sukkot* (aka, The Festival of Booths or Tabernacles). This is one of the pilgrimage festivals, like Passover and Shavuot (Pentecost), when Jews traveled to Jerusalem to celebrate. The festival's history provides a framework for some of the debates that ensue over Jesus's identity. *Sukkot* traditions also serve as a thematic backdrop to some of the bold claims Jesus makes in the scene. Contemporary Christian readers often miss the depth and complexity here because we are unfamiliar with the Jewish religious symbols and allusions woven into the story. But, don't worry, I am about to provide you with information that the *original* audience would have known. Then, I will add further clarity and meaning with a rather clever staging technique (if I do say so myself).

First, the festival background. Sukkot is a multi-faceted celebration with practices that have shifted over the many millennia Jewish people have practiced it. Several elements, though, remained central until the destruction of the Second Temple:

(1) The Torah and Moses *Sukkot* contains many connections to the Torah. The background to the festival has a direct connection to the Exodus narrative and to Moses, the key figure associated with Exodus and the whole Torah. On the second day of the festival during sabbatical years, Deuteronomy was read aloud in the temple's Court of the Women to remind the people of the law and their responsibilities in the law.[5] A great importance was placed on learning the law (or hearing the law) and rejoicing in the giving of the law through Moses.

---

[5] Josephus, a first-century Jewish historian, describes the temple as having four surrounding courts: an outer court open to all people (including foreigners, but excluding women who were menstruating), a second court for all Jews and their wives (who had no impurity), a third court for purified male Jews, and a fourth one for priests (*Against Apion* 2.103–105). The second court was also known as the women's court or the Court

(2) Booths and Branches Another key component of the Festival of Booths is the actual booth or tabernacle. The regular practice for the seven- (or eight-) day holiday is to reside in a tent, usually with a roof made of grass or plants. This tradition serves as a reminder of how God rescued Israel from slavery in Egypt, then guided them and provided for them as they wandered in the wilderness. John drops several hints in this scene that strengthen the connection to the wilderness, including Jesus's speech about thirst and the repeated mention of the grumbling crowds, recalling the Israelites' grumbling in the desert.

Because Sukkot is a harvest festival, branches from plants also play a part in the festivities. Jewish oral traditions say that in the days of the Second Temple (before it was destroyed in 70 CE), priests would carry branches made of willow, palm, myrtle, and citron as they offered psalms and prayers to God, reciting over and over, "Please save us!" Then, on the last day of Sukkot, the priests would strike willow branches on the ground around the altar as a rain rite (willow branches were associated with life-giving water because they grew near rivers). The rituals with the booths and the branches speak to the salvific theme at the festival's core—remembering God's salvation in the past, rejoicing in God's providence in the present, and asking for salvific elements (life-saving rain and spiritual redemption) for the future.

(3) Water and Light At the time of Jesus's ministry, water and light played a vital role in Sukkot celebrations. First, there was a joyful rite performed every morning of Sukkot called the *Simchat Beit Hashoavah*, which means "The Rejoicing at the Place of the Water Drawing." In this folk ritual (which is not mentioned in the Torah), the priests would go down from the temple to draw water from the pool, or wellspring, of Siloam. After collecting the water, they would bring it up to the temple

---

of the Women, but it was not restricted to women and often served as the site for non-sacrificial rituals like Torah readings. See Sara Parks, Shayna Sheinfeld, and Meredith J.C. Warren, *Jewish and Christian Women in the Ancient Mediterranean* (New York: Routledge, 2022), 122.

through the Water Gate accompanied by the blowing of the shofar and other instruments. Finally, the priests would pour the water out on the altar along with the regular, daily libation of wine.

Another staple feature of the Festival of Tabernacles was light. There were giant candelabras set up in the temple courtyard throughout the festival. These luminaries held gallons of oil and used wicks made from the priests' worn-out vestments. According to tradition, they generated such intense light that it gave the city a daylight glow even in the dark of night. In addition to the stationary lights, it was said that the elders would dance and juggle torches, providing a bright spectacle of celebration. These two festival symbols, water and light, provide another link to the wilderness wanderings. God's presence guided the people with a pillar of *light* at night and the people relied on God to provide water in the desert.

Staging for the Tabernacle Scene

A director trying to communicate the symbolism implicit in this scene might rely on props and lighting to make connections between the dialogue and the symbols. Envision this: on one side of the stage a prop dominates the backdrop; it is a scroll, to represent Torah and Moses. Center stage is a four-walled tent (or booth), with various branches hanging in the front, representing the redemptive work of God for Israel in the past, present, and future. On the other side of the stage stands a menorah (candelabra) with a water jar in front of it, symbolizing the burning presence of God and the Spirit that quenches the thirst of the people.

The scene begins at the apron of the stage. The stage itself is dark and the light illuminates a group of men talking in front of the pulled curtain, stage right.[6] It is Jesus and his brothers. The brothers are

---

[6] Note: much of the dialogue in this section comes from my own loose translation of verses from John 7 and 8. You are going to have to trust me that I capture the message well and update it appropriately.

mocking Jesus, goading him into going to Jerusalem for Sukkot: "Leave here and go to Judea so that your disciples (*air quote gestures here*) can see the works you are doing. Don't hide away in secret—show yourself to the world." Jesus knows what they are doing: "You go ahead. As for me, my time has not yet come. There are people trying to kill me in Jerusalem because they hate me. That tends to happen when you testify against people's evil deeds." The brothers leave, walking toward Jerusalem in the distance. Jesus follows after them, but stealthily.

When Jesus gets to the festival, the people trying to kill him are looking for him. On stage, this group of important-looking men are standing right in front of the scroll backdrop. Meanwhile, the rest of the stage is filled with festival crowds arguing about Jesus, and whether he is legit or dangerous. The spotlight comes up on Jesus, no longer hiding, and he begins to teach. Behind him are the menorah and water jar. Another light comes up on the scroll backdrop as the important-looking men gather in front of it, saying, "How does this man have such learning, when he has never been taught?"

Jesus answers, speaking to both the actors and the audience: "My teaching is not mine but the one who sent me. Anyone who resolves to do the will of God will know whether the teaching is from God or whether I am speaking on my own." It's a subtle dig at the men who defend the law but don't recognize God's teaching when they hear it. They don't get it, so Jesus drops the subtlety: "Did not Moses give you the law? But not one of you keeps it. Why are you trying to kill me?"

The crowd, acting like the chorus in a Greek tragedy, jumps into the discussion: "You have a demon! Who is trying to kill you?" Jesus, unphased by their accusation, defends himself using a reasonable argument: "You are upset because I healed on the Sabbath, but the law of Moses (*he gestures to the scroll across the stage from him*) allows you to be circumcised on the Sabbath. Use good judgment, people!" The questions about Jesus's knowledge (where did he get this wisdom?) and the accusations over his authority (is it from God or Satan?)—come to a temporary resolution with Jesus's learned appeal to Moses and the law.

However, the debates have just begun.

The two spotlights illuminating the scroll and the menorah fade as the lights come up on center stage, drawing the audience's attention to the booth and branches backdrop. The people on stage divide into two sides and begin arguing about whether Jesus is the Messiah. Some say it cannot be him because no one is supposed to know where the messiah comes from, and they do know where Jesus comes from. Others point to Jesus's signs saying, "When the Messiah comes, will he do more signs than this man?" The ones who marvel at Jesus's signs trust in him. The redemptive context of the festival—especially the booths that recall God's deliverance and provision—have prompted the people to wonder about the messiah. Jesus has a message for those who question his origins: "I have not come on my own. But the one who sent me is true, and you do not know him. I, on the other hand, do know him because I am from him." John is building on a theme here—in order to recognize Jesus for who he is, one has to know God. Just as Jesus comes from God, so also will the knowledge and hope necessary to follow Jesus come from God.

Jesus's teaching riles up the crowd and gains some followers; onstage we see the Pharisees and the chief priests grab some of the temple police and send them to arrest Jesus. It's hard to tell if they are protecting the crowds from someone they think to be a false teacher or if they are jealous of Jesus's following. But Jesus just keeps teaching with boldness, getting more cryptic as he goes: "I will be with you a little while longer, and then I am going to him who sent me. You will search for me, but you will not find me, and where I am, you cannot come." The Jews in the temple don't understand him, but the audience might start to recognize his language from their wisdom literature. Jesus's words sound like a combination of his signature "sent from God" language and the descriptions of Wisdom (*Sophia*) in Proverbs and other Jewish literature.[7] "Then they will call upon me, but I will not answer," Woman Wisdom says in Proverbs 1:28, "They will seek me diligently but will not find me." While the temple police are literally searching for Jesus to arrest him, Jesus is more concerned with the figurative aspects of seeking and (not) finding. The lights dim on stage as the police continue to search for Jesus in the crowd.

When the lights come back up, the narrator announces that it is the last day of the festival, the great day. A spotlight shines on the candelabra and water jar as Jesus cries out, "Let anyone who is thirsty come to me, and let the one who trusts in me drink. As the Scripture has said, 'Out of the believer's heart shall flow rivers of living water.'" The narrator speaks to the audience: "Now he said this about the Spirit, which believers in him were to receive, for as yet there was no Spirit because Jesus was not yet glorified." This shift in time and subject seems abrupt but in the context of the festival, it makes sense. Jesus's words here continue the *Sophia*/Wisdom theme[8] and also speak to the water imagery of Sukkot. Just as the priest draws the living water from the pool of Siloam to pour on the temple altar, so too, will living water flow from those who trust in Jesus. John also connects water to Spirit here, a link that we have seen already in the Nicodemus conversation (being born of water and spirit) and the woman at the well (Jesus's claim to be living water as he encourages worship in spirit and truth). John introduces a central theological idea here as well: the Spirit will not come until Jesus is glorified, or until Jesus's death. We will learn more about this in Jesus's Act 4 Farewell Discourse.

Jesus's revelatory words intensify the division on stage. The crowds start to split again, one group convinced he must be the Messiah

---

[7] The personification of God's wisdom as Woman Wisdom or *Sophia* can be found in several other passages from Jewish literature, including Proverbs 8, Sirach 1:1–4, 24:8 and Wisdom of Solomon 9:1–2. The images found in these works also appear to be in the background of John's use of *logos* (or word) in the Prologue.

[8] In Proverbs 9:5, Wisdom cries out inviting people to eat her bread and drink her wine.

or at least a prophet, the other group doubtful. The temple police seem to be on the fence, but they don't arrest him, saying, "Never has anyone spoken like this!" The Pharisees ridicule the police and the believing crowd. Our friend from Act 1, Nicodemus, appears on stage as well. Surprisingly, he defends Jesus. "Our law does not judge people without a hearing, does it?" he asks the Pharisees. But they mock him too, quick to attack anyone who sides with Jesus in public.[9]

The spotlight still shines on the water jar and menorah background when Jesus speaks again, but another beam comes up on Jesus himself: "I am the light of the world. Whoever follows me will never walk in darkness but will have the light of life." Jesus doubles down on the Sukkot symbolism with this beautiful metaphor, another "I am" statement. He is claiming to be the illuminating presence of God that went before the people in the wilderness. It is a divine claim and it does not go unchallenged. The Pharisees move across stage to oppose Jesus, insisting that Jesus's own testimony about himself is invalid. To the audience, it starts to feel like another trial scene, with witnesses and prosecutors. Jesus handles the accusations with the confidence of a master defender. "My Father, the one who sent me, is my second witness and your own law says that the testimony of two witnesses is valid." The Pharisees' response opens the door for Jesus's checkmate. "Where is your Father?," they ask and Jesus's answer condemns them: "If you knew me, you would know my Father also."

The spotlight shifts from the water jar and menorah to the booths and branches placed center stage. Jesus launches into a short speech about his supernatural origins. "I am going away but where I am going, you cannot come…You are from below, I am from above, you are from this world, I am not from this world." Jesus takes a step back from his detractors, who are confused by his words, and his motion physically illustrates the dualistic imagery he uses. "When you have lifted

---

[9] Just a note: we have skipped over 7:53–8:11, the story of the woman saved from stoning. It is a later addition to the narrative so it interrupts the flow here. We will deal with it at intermission.

up the Son of Man, then you will realize that I am he (*another "I am"!*) and that I do nothing on my own." John's drama has already foreshadowed Jesus's death this way, comparing it to the bronze snake lifted up in the wilderness. The repetition of this motif solidifies the idea that Jesus's lifting up (or the crucifixion) functions like the snake on the pole—it is a healing action on the part of God for the people.

Some of the people in the Jewish crowd gather around him—these are the ones who long for God's healing and trust that Jesus speaks the truth. Jesus looks at these Jewish believers and gives them hope: "If you continue in my word, you are truly my disciples, and you will know the truth, and the truth will make you free." [The truth, as the audience will learn soon, IS Jesus]. The Jewish hearers resist these words so Jesus continues: "Everyone who commits sin is a slave to sin. The slave doesn't have a permanent place in the family but the son does. So, if the Son makes you free, you will be free indeed."

It's a great line for the end of the scene. But it's not the end. Instead, the crowds (even, it seems, the ones who had started trusting in Jesus) start to argue and debate with Jesus. They claim that their Abrahamic ancestry gives them understanding, but Jesus insists that if they followed Abraham and were children of God, they would love him (Jesus), whom God sent. Then Jesus levels a critique against the crowds, one that would fuel a host of scapegoating atrocities against Jewish people later in history. "Why do you not understand what I say?" Jesus laments, "It is because you cannot accept my word. You are from your father, the devil, and you choose to do your father's desires. He was a murderer from the beginning and does not stand in the truth because there is no truth in him. When he lies, he speaks according to his own nature, for he is a liar and the father of lies calls them illegitimate children who follow their father the devil, who is a liar" (8:43–44).

We need to pause here: this harsh insult functions as a literary device that John uses hyperbolically against people, known elsewhere in John as "the world", who don't understand Jesus (or would not accept who the *logos* really is, a group foreshadowed in 1:11). It is not a condemnation of every Jewish person and it does not imply that Jewish people are evil. Anti-Jewish church fathers used it this way as did those who scapegoated Jews for the Bubonic plague and countless other disasters right up to the present day. They were and are wrong. Jesus was a Jew living and teaching among his fellow Jews. The group he is speaking to in this scene are his people. Although it is possible that in John's late first-century context there could have been tensions between Jewish and Christian groups that influenced such hyperbole, we cannot take the words here as a condemnation of Jewish people as a whole, any more than we would condemn all Christians if the pastor of a wealthy congregation called out her church for their neglect of the poor. These words serve as polemical rhetoric to awaken the audience to the truth of Jesus's teaching, to convince them to trust Jesus.[10]

Jesus is much more concerned with convincing the crowds to turn to him than he is with condemning them. With his next breath, he cajoles them, "Whoever is from God hears the words of God," but the people in the temple don't fall for his lure. Instead, they call him a Samaritan and demon (an appropriate response to his inciting insult?). In response, Jesus doubles down on his persuasive language. "Whoever keeps my word will never taste death." There is silence on stage as they stare at him, flabbergasted. Then they scoff, claiming even Abraham died. Finally, Jesus brings the debate in the temple to an end, "Very truly, I tell you, before Abraham was, I AM!"

And with that "I am" statement resounding through the air, the people on stage pick up stones to throw at him. The conflict at the festival has turned violent. Before the stage goes dark, we see Jesus slip off stage, escaping the temple scene. He's safe—but not for long.

---

[10] I think the way that Jo-Ann Brant explains it helps us separate the readers' context from our own: "Demonizing one's opponent when one is powerless, as early Christians were, is a protest against one's status, but demonizing them when one stands in a position of power or when one knows that such words can incite violence is considered a hate crime in many modern nations." See Brant, *John*, 149.

CHAPTER FIVE

Intermission
& Bonus Scene

After you visit the concessions during intermission and make your way back from the lobby, you realize there is a stripped-down scene being acted on stage. It is not part of the main drama; they haven't even flickered the lights to end intermission. It's a bonus scene, in fact, one not officially included in any of the acts. As you watch, though, you realize that its themes fit in with those from the last scene: the episode is set in the temple, Jesus is teaching, the religious leaders are trying to get Jesus arrested, and someone is in danger of being stoned. The author of this short passage thinks much like a stage director would, making more use of space and posture than dialogue or exposition. This makes it the perfect candidate for a dramatic retelling. As the scene unfolds, notice how the staging plays a role in how the author communicates the nuances of the story, especially Jesus's posture. We will discuss this more after the story. So, settle back in your plush chair and enjoy this bonus scene, The Woman Saved from Stoning, before we return to the main action of John's narrative.[1]

---

[1] Why is the "woman caught in adultery" story (I call it "the woman saved from stoning" story) a bonus scene? Early manuscripts of John's Gospel do not contain this episode, so it is unlikely to have been part of the original storyline. Manuscript evidence shows that it appears in various places throughout Luke and John during the first centuries of the church, as if scribes

The lights flood the stage and we see Jesus sitting on some steps, stage right, facing the audience with his hands poised as if in the middle of teaching them. The scribes and Pharisees enter from stage left as a group, making a ruckus with their entrance and dragging a woman behind him. The woman looks terrified as the scribes and Pharisees roughly push her so she is downstage center, displayed before Jesus, the crowd, and the audience. One of them speaks up: "Teacher, this woman was caught in the *very act* of committing adultery. Now, in the law Moses commanded us to stone such women. So, what do *you* say?"

The narrator's voice floats in from the wings, stage-whispering an explanation: "They said this to test him, so that they might have some charge to bring against him." Jesus makes a show of looking around to see if they have brought any other offenders with them—the man caught in the act, perhaps. But there is no *man caught in the very act of adultery* in this scene, despite the law's stipulation that both the man and woman caught in adultery should be stoned. Once Jesus sees this, he shakes his head. There is silence on the stage for several moments while the audience waits on the edges of their seats to hear what Jesus is going to say. But Jesus says nothing. Instead, he slowly bends down and uses his finger to write on the stage floor. The gazes of the Pharisees,

---

were trying it out in different contexts. Gail O'Day ("John 7:53–8:11: A Study in Misreading," *Journal of Biblical Literature* 111: 631–40) suggests the church fathers were uncomfortable with the leniency Jesus shows to an adulteress because of their emphasis on chastity (and probably their latent, historically-dictated sexism) and so it could have been purposefully left out or moved around. A textual-critical study by Jennifer Knust and Tommy Wasserman tells a different story, insisting the story was beloved and flexible, used in a variety of ways in the early church (*To Cast the First Stone: The Transmission of a Gospel Story* [Princeton, NJ: Princeton University Press], 2018). Frances Taylor Gench (*Back to the Well: Women's Encounters with Jesus in the Gospels* [Louisville, KY: Westminster John Knox Press, 2004], 136–59) maintains that because this passage continued to find its way into different contexts in the Gospels, it is likely authentic, and was an important piece of the first Christians' remembrances of Jesus that needed a narrative home.

scribes, and the gathered crowd follow Jesus and they appear to be perplexed.

The religious leaders break the silence with a barrage of protests, impatiently hounding Jesus for an answer. "What do you say?" "Tell us!" "Do you disregard the law?" "The law commands it!," "Answer us!" Jesus straightens slowly and looks at the crowd around him and the religious men who seem out for blood. His eyes linger on the ones who brought the woman to him, but his next words seem to be addressed to the whole crowd. "Let anyone among you who is without sin be the first to throw a stone at her." His words hang in the air and from the audience, there are gasps of awe and realization as the brilliance of his answer settles in. After the initial shock seems to wear off, Jesus crouches down once more and writes on the ground. All eyes are again on Jesus and the crowd stands in uncomfortable silence. Then they slowly begin to walk away, one by one, until all have exited to the wings. The only people left on stage are the woman and Jesus. A man and a woman alone. The ancient audience would understand the shocking significance of the moment because a man and woman who were not related did not stand together or talk to each other in public. In fact, if they had and the women was married, she could be accused of adultery. Jesus does not seem concerned with social taboos, however. His attention is on the woman.

Jesus raises himself from the ground and takes an almost imperceptible step forward, leaning in to speak gently and quietly to her. "Woman, where are they? Has no one condemned you?" The woman raises her head, which has been lowered the whole time she had been on stage. She meets Jesus's eyes and says, "No one, sir." Jesus smiles. "Then neither do I condemn you. Go your way and from now on, do not sin again." He nods his head in the direction that the scribes and Pharisees exited, as if to say, "Keep away from their scrutiny, especially." The woman backs slowly away from Jesus, trying to keep him in her sight until she disappears offstage.

Jesus's posture and actions play a key role in the author's narration of this scene. When the scribes and Pharisees approach Jesus, he is teaching, probably sitting on some steps in front of a small crowd. After they bring their accusations before him, Jesus bends down (perhaps descending the steps) to write or draw on the ground. This is Jesus's first change in posture and it draws the shaming gazes of the crowd to what he is etching on the ground, effectively drawing attention away from the woman, whom the religious leaders have centered in their drama of condemnation.[2] His movement out of a sitting position, a posture typical for rabbinic teaching but also indicative of divine judgment, may indicate that Jesus has chosen not to judge the woman, as the religious leaders are pushing him to do.

After Jesus stoops, he writes something on the ground. Scholars and pastors have spent much effort trying to reconstruct this unrecoverable detail. But the words do not seem to be the focus of the author. If Jesus had inscribed the sins of the accusers or the prohibitions from the Ten Commandments, we would have been told this. If he had drawn a picture, written a verse, or posed a probing, rhetorical question, the writers probably would have let the audience in on that detail. It is not *what* Jesus writes that is important, but *what effect* his writing has. Jesus scratching in the dirt serves as a distraction to the accusers, pulling them from their path of violence and directing their focus AWAY from the object of condemnation.

Jesus's second change of posture comes when he straightens up and turns his attention from the ground to the scribes and Pharisees. A director blocking this scene might pull Jesus forward at this point, to sharpen the audience's focus on Jesus and allow his shape to dominate the other characters on stage. When Jesus bends to write on the ground once again, there is a third change of posture. Now, the focus of the audience and the accusers remains on Jesus, but his words encouraging self-reflection shift the judgment of the crowd onto themselves. Jesus's

---

[2] Alicia D. Myers, *Reading John and 1, 2, 3 John: A Literary and Theological Commentary* (Macon, GA: Smyth & Helwys, 2019), 108.

pause gives them time to soul search and they realize they cannot stand in condemnation of the woman until they confront their own guilt. Jesus has turned them away from their violent intent by opening their eyes to their own culpability. The woman, representative of so many women who have become sexual scapegoats for religious groups, is no longer the sinner in the story.[3] The accusers and their mob-in-the-making now condemn themselves as they walk away.

Jesus's final change of posture is perhaps the most important of all. He straightens up again and directly addresses the woman who, up until this point in the story, has been treated as an object, a scapegoat for religious leaders and a pawn in their plan to trap Jesus. His last words are two rhetorical questions that restore the woman's dignity and free her from society's condemnation: "Woman, where are they? Has no one condemned you?" When the scene ends, the would-be judge and the woman accused are face-to-face, standing on the equal ground that Jesus has created for them.

END OF INTERMISSION

---

[3] For more on women as scapegoats in the church, see the first section of my book, *Scapegoats: The Gospel through the Eyes of Victims* (Minneapolis, MN: Fortress Press), 2022.

CHAPTER SIX

Act 3: John 9–12
Light, Life, & the Pursuit
of Salvation

CHARACTERIZATIONS OF JESUS
The Son of Man | The one who gives sight to the blind |
The Good Shepherd | The Gate | The Resurrection and Life | The Way

SUPPORTING CHARACTERS
The man healed from blindness | The man's parents |
Mary, Martha, and Lazarus | The divided crowds | Caiaphas and Jewish
authorities | The disciples

Scene 1: At Last, I See the Light (John 9)

The curtain rises for the second half of John's drama with the threat of violence still palpable. Before the intermission, Jesus had barely escaped being stoned in the temple, and in the bonus scene we witnessed another stoning incident, this one with a woman at the center of the violence. Although Act 3 starts more calmly—Jesus taking

ACT 3 PLAYLIST

Scene 1

"And at Last I See the Light" from *Tangled*

Scene 2

"Where Have All the Flowers Gone?" by Peter, Paul, and Mary

Scene 3

"Seasons of Love" from *Rent*, "Lazarus" by David Bowie

Scene 4

"You Raise Me Up" by Josh Groban

a leisurely stroll with his disciples—the theater goers know the story is moving ever closer to bloodshed.

On their walk, Jesus and his disciples come upon a man who was born blind. The disciples voice a common idea concerning illness and disability in the ancient world: "Rabbi, who sinned, this man or his parents, that he was born blind?" Jesus's answer, as rendered by most English-language Bibles, reveals the theologies of disability held by contemporary translators: "Neither this man nor his parents sinned; he was born blind so that God's works might be revealed in him. We must work the works of him who sent me while it is day" (NRSVue). In this translation, it is implied that God caused the man's blindness so that one day he could become a miraculous sign of Jesus's power. Good news for the man, right? His suffering serves a higher purpose—it is all part of God's master plan.

Only, that's an iffy translation of the Greek, says John scholar Alicia Myers. Translators usually add in the phrase "he was born blind" to separate the first half of the sentence from the second part. Myers's translation factors in the lack of punctuation in the original Greek without adding a phrase that manipulates the meaning. She translates it this way: "Neither this one sinned nor his parents; but so that the works of God might be revealed to him it is necessary for us to work the works of the one who sent me while it is daytime." That's a pretty big difference. It demonstrates that translation is not a science; it's an art. And it's an art form that involves enough interpretive guesswork that it can be easily molded to fit cultural assumptions or pre-existing theological convictions.

As Jesus walks over to the man, he repeats the imagery taken from the Festival of Booths: "I am the light of the world." The first time

Jesus referred to himself as light, he drew on symbolism from the exodus wanderings—the light of God's presence guiding the Israelites out of the wilderness. Now, he takes a more tactile approach. He gets on the ground, makes mud with his saliva, and spreads the concoction on the man's eyes. He is going to make this guy see the light—literally. He instructs the man to go wash in the pool of Siloam (yes, the same one from the *Sukkot* water ritual), and the man comes back healed.

This healing is one of the signs John chooses to narrate—miracles that point to a deeper meaning about Jesus's identity. In the same way that the wedding at Cana sign reveals Jesus as the abundantly generous host of the messianic banquet and the sign of the feeding of the 5,000 shows Jesus as a nourishing provider who gives his own body as food, the sign in John 9 demonstrates that Jesus is the giver of sight and revealer of truth. Jesus's healing of the man born with blindness is either the fifth or the sixth sign (out of seven) in John's Gospel. It is difficult to tell which sign it is mainly because the author stops counting after the second sign and scholars disagree about whether Jesus walking on water is its own sign or is part of the feeding of the 5,000. Let's call it the sixth sign, because I am of the opinion that the raising of Lazarus, the next sign, is the seventh sign rather than Jesus's resurrection.[1] This sixth sign

---

[1] Scholars who count this as the fifth sign will call the raising of Lazarus the sixth sign and the resurrection of Jesus the seventh. The problem with this numeration is twofold: thematically speaking, the signs in John are miracles performed by Jesus to reveal pieces of his identity. The resurrection of Jesus is not done by Jesus, nor does it reveal something about him, as the raising of Lazarus sign is when Jesus calls himself "the resurrection and the life." Literarily, the second part of John's Gospel has a different feel than the first part. The first part has often been called "The Book of Signs" and the second part "The Book of Glory," because the former speaks more about Jesus's public signs and teachings, while the latter narrates Jesus's private teachings with the disciples and his journey to the cross. Naming the raising of Lazarus as the seventh sign makes it the climax of the Book of Signs and a turning point in the narrative. For all these reasons, I prefer to call this sign the sixth and Lazarus the seventh.

causes quite the stir because Jesus heals the man on the Sabbath, just as he did with the man by the pool.

After the miracle, the scene proceeds in little vignettes, discreet interrogations that grow in intensity.

Neighbor's Vignette: The lights come up stage right and we see the healed man next to some of his neighbors who are beginning to argue. "Isn't this the guy who used to sit and beg?" They gesture to him as if he were a park bench, obtrusive and inanimate. Some neighbors say, "Yeah, that's him." Others disagree, "No, it just looks like him." The man keeps trying to interject: "I am (the one)," he repeats (and yep, that's *ego eimi*, like Jesus's "I am" statements). The neighbors finally hear him and began badgering him: "Then how were your eyes opened?" Even after the man recounts the story about the mud, spit and the pool, they remain dubious. "Where is he?," they ask. "I don't know." The man's words end the vignette and the lights go down.

Pharisee's Vignette #1: The lights come up stage left and we see the neighbors drag the man to a group of Jewish religious leaders. The Pharisees, upset once more about a healing on the Sabbath, interrogate the man about how he received his sight. He explains again, "He put mud on my eyes. Then I washed, and now I see." His answer starts to divide the Pharisees as it did the neighbors. Some say, "This man is not from God, for he does not observe the Sabbath." Others say, "How can a man who is a sinner perform such signs?"

"What do you say about him?" the interrogators turn their attention back to the healed man.

"He is a prophet," the man declares. Apparently, this guy has more guts than the man healed at the pool. The lights flash bright for a moment and then go dark.

Parents' Vignette: The darkness persists for several seconds and then we hear the narrator's voice: "The Jews did not believe that he had been blind and had received his sight until they called the parents of the man who had received his sight." The lights come up stage right and we see a group of people interrogating a nervous couple. "Is this your son, who you say was born blind? How then does he now see?" The man's parents answer, "We know that this is our son and that he was born blind, but we do not know how it is that now he sees, nor do we know who opened his eyes. Ask him; he is of age. He will speak for himself."

The lights cut off abruptly to punctuate the parents' dismissive response. The narrator ends the vignette as he began it: "They said this because they were afraid of the Jews, for the Jews had already agreed that anyone who confessed Jesus to be the Messiah would be put out of the synagogue." [Here is a spot in the text where we see the two-level narrative at play. It is so unlikely that, during the lifetime of Jesus, people were being thrown out of the synagogue for "confessing" Jesus as Messiah that scholars tend to explain this line as more likely describing the contemporary context of John's original writer and readers.]

Pharisee's Vignette #2: The house lights come up and the religious leaders have moved to the floor, bringing the interrogation scene into the audience. They cry out, "Give glory to God! We know that the man Jesus is a sinner." The healed man shakes his head: "I don't know if he's a sinner. One thing I do know, I once was blind, but now I see." They ask him to repeat the story of the healing and the man is, understandably, done with the interrogation. "I have told you already, and you would not listen." He smirks sarcastically at them. "Why do you want to hear it again? Do you also want to become his disciples?"

"You are his disciple," the religious men point at him, "but we are disciples of Moses." They draw their shoulders back with pride. "We know that God has spoken to Moses, but as for this man, we do not know where he comes from."

The man is on a roll now and he starts to draw the audience in with his bold subversion. "What an astonishing thing! You don't know where he comes from, yet he opened my eyes. We know that God does not listen to sinners, but to those who worship and obey...If this man were not from God, he could do nothing." Some people in the audience start to clap but the religious men cut them off. "You were born entirely in sins, and are you trying to teach us?" The insult is aimed at the man who had been blind, but some audience members draw back as if slapped. The leaders grab the man and force him away from the audience and out a side door. The house lights go back down.

Jesus's Vignette: An overhead light shines on center stage as if from the heavens and we see Jesus approaching the healed man for the first time since the sign. "Do you believe in the Son of Man?" Jesus asks him, but the question feels more like a secret revelation than an interrogation. The man responds, "And who is he? Tell me, so that I may believe in him." Jesus gives him a knowing nod: "You're looking at him right now" (my translation).

The man who had been blind falls to his knees and utters the next words as quiet as a prayer, "Lord, I believe." Jesus looks out to the audience and delivers the climactic statement, "I came into this world for judgment, so that those who do not see may see," he gestures to the healed man, "and those who do see may become blind." Jesus nods his head at a group of Pharisees who are walking across the stage toward him. The interrogators look indignant, "Surely we are not blind, are we?" Jesus lays down the ironic truth, more for the sake of the audience than the religious men. "If you were blind, you would not have sin. But now that you say, 'We see,' your sin remains." The center stage light blinks off. And…scene.

You might have noticed that while Jesus starts this scene by healing the man born blind (9:1–7), he disappears from the stage for the neighbors' interrogation (vv 8–12), the Pharisees' questioning (vv 13–17), the interrogation of the parents (vv 18–23), and the Pharisees' final argument with the man (vv 24–34). These four vignettes form the longest passage in the Gospels without Jesus in it, aside from the infancy narratives. It is an odd omission for John, who has focused so intensely on Jesus's presence and work—why would the Light of the World leave the stage for so long?

According to Jo-Ann Brant, a Johannine scholar at Goshen College, Jesus does not completely leave the stage here. She points out that John 9 employs a literary device that would later be called *mise en abyme*. This technique, used today in art, film, and advertising, is also known as the "Droste effect" after a cocoa powder ad that featured a miniature version of its product and logo on its logo picture. You may be more familiar with a contemporary version of this effect if you know the butter brand, Land O'Lakes: their logo used to have a stereotypically-clad Native American holding a package of Land O'Lakes butter displaying the label and the same picture of the stereotypically-clad Native American holding a package of Land O'Lakes butter displaying the label...and so on. It is an ad within an ad, a picture within a picture. This is how the story of the man with blindness functions—as a miniature version of the larger story of Jesus, or a mirror story within a story. The narrative of the healed man parallels Jesus's narrative in many ways, including the following: the crowd questions his identity (9:8–9), he asserts "I am" (9:9), he speaks frankly and logically throughout but is treated as an invalid witness (9:18), he is accused of being a sinner, and he combats the Pharisees with sarcasm and truth (9:34).[2]

This story within the story heightens the ironic punchline of the episode—that those who think they can see are blind to the truth while the one who was blind (and a "sinner" and accused of being an invalid witness) is the one who sees. The *mise en abyme* also provides the audience with a glimpse at how followers of Jesus might go on after he has left the stage of earth: like the healed man, they should imitate Jesus as a bold witness to the truth despite opposition.

---

[2] Jo-Ann Brant, *John*, Paideia: Commentaries on the New Testament (Grand Rapids, MI: Baker Academic, 2011), 155.

Scene 2: The Shepherd Sings and the Sheep Scatter (John 10)

The next scene starts and Jesus is sitting downstage on a stool, strumming a guitar. The song he plays, sung to the tune of Peter, Paul and Mary's (wink wink) "Where Have all the Flowers Gone," adds an intimate edge to the message he will bring.

I come through the sheepfold gate
I am the Shepherd
The sheep hear my voice and know
I am their Shepherd
I call my sheep by name
And lead them out to graze
Oh, when will you learn my voice?
Oh, when will you...follow me?

I am the Good Shepherd
I'll give my life for you
The wolves come, but never fear
I won't let them harm you
I am your Good Shepherd
I know you and you know me
Does not the Father know me?
Don't I know our...Father too?

My sheep hear me, not the thieves
I am the sheep gate
Come through me and you'll be safe
I'll find you pasture
The thief comes to steal and kill
I came to give you life
Will you abundantly live?
Will you have life...to the full?

I lay down my life for you
And for my other sheep
They hear my voice calling out
I'll bring them also
So one day we'll unify
One flock, one shepherd
For this won't I give my life?
For this won't I take it back?

I rendered this content as a simple song but in John, it appears as a parable-like speech often known as the Good Shepherd discourse. The discourse is not a parable, that teaching form we see saturating the Synoptic Gospels, but is instead a *paroimia*, a Greco-Roman rhetorical device that functions like a fable or allegory. A *paroimia* uses upbeat words and images to communicate serious subject matter. A folk song introduced into this tense, debate/division section (John 5–12) would hit the same way a *paroimia* did in the ancient world. It provides a brief and entertaining respite from the conflict, just as John designed.[3] We jump right back into it, though, because after Jesus's shepherd teaching, John tells us: "Again the Jews were divided because of these words. Many of them were saying, 'He has a demon and is out of his mind. Why listen to him?' Others were saying, 'These are not the words of one who has a demon. Can a demon open the eyes of the blind?'"

In the middle of chapter 10, John rockets the audience forward to another festival, this time it's the Festival of the Dedication (or Hanukkah). Jesus is in Jerusalem again and the Jewish people there are still divided about his messianic identity. The debate sounds familiar, touching on themes from the Good Shepherd speech, the Tabernacles debacle, and the healing at the pool.

Jews: "How long will you keep us in suspense? If you are the Messiah, just tell us so!"

Jesus: "I have told you, and you do not have faith. The works that I do in my Father's name testify to me, but you do not trust because you do not belong to my sheep—you know, the ones who hear my voice and follow me. These are the ones I will give eternal life; they will never be snatched out of my hand or the Father's hand. Because, remember, the Father and I are one."

Jews: Alright, surely now we can stone him. *They reach for some stones.*

Jesus: I have shown you many good works from the Father. For which of these are you going to stone me? *Mic drop.*

Jews: It is not for a good work that we are going to stone you but for blasphemy, because you—though only a human—are making yourself God.

---

[3] See Brant, 160.

Jesus: You say that the one the Father has sanctified and sent into the world (that's me) is blaspheming because I said, 'I am God's Son'? If I am not doing the works of my Father, then don't trust in me. But if I do them, even though you do not believe me, trust the works, so that you may know and understand that the Father is in me and I am in the Father.

John tells us that in the aftermath of this debate, the Jerusalem Jews unsuccessfully try to arrest Jesus again, and he escapes across the Jordan to the place where John had been baptizing earlier. Okay, so we're revisiting the witness to the light, now? Well played, authors. The people's claim in 10:41 that "John performed no sign, but everything that John said about this man was true," ties this second half of John to the first half quite well. John ends this scene with an optimistic assessment of the people across the Jordan (in contrast to the ones who rejected Jesus in Jerusalem): "And many trusted in him there."[4]

So, for now we know that the Good Shepherd song rings true: there are some sheep who hear Jesus's voice and they will have life. But there are other sheep who have scattered because they don't recognize their shepherd. The audience must be wondering, "Which one am I?," which is exactly what John intended.

Scene 3: Love, Death, and Resuscitation (John 11:1–12:8)

I have a multitude of favorite scenes in the Gospel of John, but this one may be my actual favorite. The story of Mary, Martha, and Lazarus is a climactic one in the Gospel of John, in several ways. First, it is an emotional and relational climax for Jesus. The whole passage

---

[4] Recall my omitted scene from Act 1 in which John the Baptist is downplayed, emphasized as a witness to the light, the friend of the bridegroom. It was in a footnote so you might have missed it.

is saturated with emotional responses and although such expression would be common in Jewish funeral practices, the fact that John uses the affective demonstrations from the beginning of the chapter (well before the scene at the tomb) is significant. Thus far in the narrative, Jesus has been characterized in a more aloof way, affected only minimally by those around him (see 2:24—"Jesus would not entrust himself to them…"). But here, we encounter the following emotional and relational descriptions, most of them referring to Jesus:

- "he whom you love" (from the sisters' message to Jesus in 11:3)
- "Jesus loved Martha and her sister and Lazarus" (11:5)
- "our friend" (Jesus says about Lazarus in 11:11)
- console/consoling (11:19 and 11:31)
- weeping (the Jews, Mary, and Jesus in 11:31–35)
- "[Jesus] was greatly disturbed in spirit and deeply moved" (11:33)
- "See, how he loved him!" (The Jews say of Jesus in 11:36).

There is arguably no other scene in the Gospels where Jesus is as relationally and emotionally connected to people than in John 11. Jesus loves his dear friends, is deeply moved, and even weeps. As the story moves on from here, Jesus's interactions with his disciples show increasing relationality and affection (see the foot-washing scene and Jesus's farewell address). This scene seems to serve as a catalyst for Jesus opening himself up more to humanity.

Appropriately, then, the theatrical version of this episode will unfold in an intimate way. No upbeat songs or dancing, no clamor or chaos, just sorrow conveyed through muted tones from the orchestra and vulnerable performances on stage. The scene might begin with Jesus and the disciples approaching Bethany, where Jesus's friends are lamenting the unthinkable loss of their brother.

The disciples, tired from a long journey, speak quietly amongst themselves: "Why would he hear about his friend's illness and then make us wait days to leave?," "I know he said Lazarus would be alright, but he's said cryptic things like that before," "I am getting more nervous every step we take toward Jerusalem; I've got a bad feeling about this." They stop their chatter as a woman walks across the stage toward them.

It's Martha, sister of the deceased, her eyes full of tears. "Lord, if you had been here, my brother would not have died." It is an accusation as much as it is an acknowledgement of Jesus's power, but Martha leans into the hope of that power. "Even now I know that God will give you whatever you ask of him." She raises her gaze to his, desperation and grief etched on her face.

Jesus says, "Your brother will rise again." Martha nods but replies tentatively, as if trying to gauge his meaning. "I know...that he will rise again in the resurrection on the last day." Jesus neither confirms or denies her claim, saying instead: "I am the resurrection and the life. Those who trust in me, even though they die, will live, and everyone who lives and trusts in me will never die. Do you believe this?" This "I am" statement is a watershed moment of self-revelation in John, another climax in the story. The concepts in the statement point backward and forward in the narrative: there is a reflection on the earlier theme of life (Jesus as the "life" in the Prologue and then offering eternal and abundant life) and a foreshadowing of Jesus's own resurrection on the horizon.

Martha's response is no less climactic; her words form the Christological confession that unlocks John's narrative: "Yes, Lord, I trust that you are the *Messiah, the Son of God*, the one coming into the world." The narrator will tell us later that the signs in this book "are written so that you may have faith that Jesus is the *Messiah, the Son of God*, and that through trusting you may have life in his name" (20:31). Although it is Peter who gives the Christological confession in the Synoptic Gospels, Martha provides the climax of confession here, using the Johannine vocabulary of trust or faith.[5] This detail should not

---

[5] Christological confession simply means a statement or affirmation that Jesus is the Messiah, or Christ. The Christological confession Peter gives can be found in Mark 8:27–30, Matt 16:13–20 and Luke 9:18–21. In it, Peter answers Jesus's question about who people were saying he was with the confession, "You are the Messiah."

be overlooked. When John holds up a woman as the model of faith and discipleship, it alerts us to the existence (and importance) of women disciples in Jesus's ministry and early Christian communities.[6]

Speaking of women disciples, Mary now crosses the stage to Jesus, a crowd of grieving neighbors and friends trailing behind her. She falls to the ground at Jesus's feet and repeats her sister's words, "Lord, if you had been here, my brother would not have died." The narrator's voice fills in the silence that follows Mary's accusation: "When Jesus saw her weeping and the Jews who came with her also weeping, he was greatly disturbed in spirit and deeply moved." Perhaps witnessing the abject sorrow and tremulous faith of both his friends was what finally broke Jesus's composure.

Jesus himself begins to cry then and if we haven't yet reached for our tissues, we do now. Jesus—the Word, provider of bread and truth, light of the world, vigilant shepherd, the very source of life itself—sheds creaturely tears for his friends and for the plight of all humanity. The streaks of compassion and pain on Jesus's face demonstrate why

---

[6] Exciting research has recently uncovered new theories on Mary Magdalene's role in the Gospel story. Elizabeth Schrader and Joan Taylor have researched manuscripts and early patristic sources and they argue (convincingly) that the Mary in this scene is Mary Magdalene (this Mary was not "from Magdala" but was known as Mary "the Tower," the translation of *magdala*). Mary the Tower is the Johannine counterpart to Peter the Rock and she may be the only woman originally in this scene. Martha, they argue, is a character added later to diminish the importance of Mary the Tower. If this is true, Mary gives the Christological confession here (not Martha), anoints Jesus for his death, and is the key disciple to witness the resurrection. Her importance has been covered up because of—you guessed it—patriarchy. Since this is such recent research, the information is in article form. If you have access to an online theological library, you can look these articles up there: Elizabeth Schrader and Joan E. Taylor, "The Meaning of "Magdalene": A Review of Literary Evidence," *Journal of Biblical literature*, Vol.140.4 (2021), 751-773 and Elizabeth Schrader, "Was Martha of Bethany Added to the Fourth Gospel in the Second Century?," *The Harvard Theological Review*, Vol.110. 3 (2017), 360-392. Or listen to "Resurrecting Mary the Tower with Elizabeth Schrader Polczer," episode 245 of The Bible for Normal People podcast.

incarnation is not just an idea—it is a revolution. Through Jesus, the divine experiences the power of human friendship, the resilience of family bonds, and the sting of mortal death. And because the human one also has the power of resurrection and life, the grave is not the end of the story.

Martha and Jesus walk upstage, to a back corner where a large stone is half-visible to the audience. The whole tomb remains off stage. Martha protests about the smell of the corpse, but Jesus does not let it stop him. He commands the people near the tomb to take away the stone. Jesus then raises his gaze to the rafters and voices a peculiar but thematically-Johannine prayer: "Father, I thank you for having heard me. I knew that you always hear me, but I have said this for the sake of the crowd standing here, so that they may trust that you sent me." Then, in a voice that punches through the veil of shadow and death, Jesus cries, "Lazarus, come out!" A man hobbles out of the darkness of the stage wings, appearing to emerge from the tomb entrance. His hands and feet are bound, his face wrapped in a cloth. Very *Night of the Living Dead*. Jesus tells the people standing around, "Unbind him, and let him go," and although he's clearly referring to Lazarus, those of us in the audience get the feeling that, on some level, he is speaking about us.

This powerfully narrated *resuscitation* scene (not *resurrection* because presumably Lazarus eventually dies and resurrection is technically a permanent state) offers the audience a glimpse of the coming drama. John purposely structures the episode to foreshadow Jesus's resurrection scene: women disciples are gathered at a tomb, a stone is rolled away, a Mary is weeping. Even the words Jesus says in 11:34, "Where have you laid him?" prefigure the words Mary Magdalene will say at the garden tomb, "Tell me where you have laid him." The eerily matching details have prompted more than one scholar to suggest that the Lazarus story is a literary creation, not a historical event. It's not an outlandish suggestion. Despite the pivotal part it plays in John's plot as Jesus's seventh and final sign and the catalyst for Jesus's arrest, this miracle does not appear in the Synoptics. But, I told you at the beginning that we are primarily pursuing matters of story here, not history, so let's get on with that.[7]

As I mentioned, the raising of Lazarus serves as the last straw for the Jewish authorities. Many Jews trust in Jesus after they witness his spectacular seventh sign, but some go to the Pharisees to tattle. The chief priests and scribes express concern about Jesus's power: "What are we to do? This man is performing many signs. If we let him go on like this, everyone will believe in him, and the Romans will come and destroy both our holy place and our nation." Their concern may have been warranted: Judea was a hotbed of revolt at that time and the Jewish leaders, along with Roman representatives and soldiers, were tasked with quelling rebellion. If Jesus gathered enough followers and stormed Jerusalem, it could end in destruction for the Jews.

The high priest, Caiaphas, responds to their fear with a practical but perverse explanation: "You do not understand that it is better for you to have one man die for the people than to have the whole nation destroyed." The narrator gives his interpretation of Caiaphas's scape-goat plan: apparently, this priest was prophesying Jesus would die for the nation, which would gather together the dispersed children of God as well. This scene gives us a glimpse of the larger picture of both Jesus's context and the context of John's audience. In Jesus's context, it is true that the Jewish people were nervous about the power and presence of Rome. They were at the mercy of the empire and their central place of worship, the Jerusalem Temple, was vulnerable to destruction if the Jews stepped out of line. A revolt during Passover instigated by people

---

[7] Okay, fine, we can talk a little bit about history but not because we can prove anything. A common contemporary explanation is that the Lazarus story could not be historical; if it had been, we would have read something about it in the other Gospels or elsewhere. I am not a modernist so I am open to the resuscitation having happened in some way, shape, or form, and maybe Lazarus was still living when the Synoptic Gospels were written so they left it out because they did not want to draw dangerous attention to him (a plausible but hypothetical suggestion). We really don't know the historical event behind this story, if there is one. I am much more concerned with what the authors are trying to do literarily with this scene. And you should be, too.

who followed Jesus would have been a worst-case scenario for those who wanted to keep the peace and their power in the Roman system (specifically, the temple authorities and Jewish political and religious rulers). John's audience in the late first century, however, would have already experienced the destruction of the temple by the Romans in 70 CE and so this statement would have been ironic. The death of Jesus around 30 CE did not prevent the destruction of the temple in 70 CE.

This death-ridden but hope-soaked scene doesn't end with enemies plotting Jesus's arrest but with disciples preparing Jesus for his upcoming death. The description of Mary anointing Jesus is strange because it clashes with parallel episodes in the Synoptic Gospels. Not quite the anointing scene from Mark (Mk 14:3–9) and not quite the Mary and Martha scene from Luke (Lk 10:38–42), this hodgepodge incident at Lazarus's home shows Martha serving her guests and Mary pouring expensive nard on Jesus's feet so she could wipe them with her hair. John turns this beautiful act of devotion into a vehicle for his vilification of Judas. On stage, Jesus would be front center, reclining on a cushion on the ground while Mary kneels at his feet. Mary fills the house with the smell of perfume, but the next part of the scene assaults the audience with the stench of betrayal.

Judas Iscariot—who we learn is about to hand Jesus over to the authorities—whines, "Why was this perfume not sold for three hundred denarii and the money given to the poor?" The narrator pulls no punches with his aggressive aside: "He said this not because he cared about the poor but because he was a thief; he kept the common purse and used to steal what was put into it." Alright, so maybe our authors are holding onto a grudge when it comes to Judas. Fortunately, Jesus's words are the ones we are left with. "Leave her alone. She bought it so that she might keep it for the day of my burial. You always have the poor with you, but you do not always have me."[8] And with that morbid

---

[8] Side note: this saying of Jesus–"you always have the poor with you, but you do not always have me" (one that also appears in Mark 14:7 and Matthew 26:11)–is NOT a prediction that there will always be poor people and so we

prediction hanging awkwardly in the air, the scene ends and we turn our attention to Jerusalem and Jesus's last week with his disciples.

Scene 4: Save Us, Jesus! But Not that Way... (the Rest of John 12)

The transition from Scene 3 to Scene 4 is a jarring one. When the lights go down on the intimate anointing scene, the narrator warns us that Jesus's act of resuscitation has endangered not only Jesus's life but Lazarus's as well. When the lights come back up, it's the next day in Jerusalem. A mass of pilgrims gathering for the Passover festival flood the stage, shouting and wielding palm branches. "Hosanna!" they cry. (Please, save!) They've come to meet Jesus as he enters the city, in much the same way as Greek and Roman citizens would receive a civic leader, and the snippet of Scripture with which they greet Jesus makes it clear that they want him to be their Messiah and king. The crowd quotes a psalm used in ancient Israel to welcome the king, their deliverer—"Blessed is the one who comes in the name of the Lord" (Ps 118:26); they even add their own title at the end to solidify Jesus's kingship—"the King of Israel!" Then, John describes how Jesus responds to the crowd's desire to make him king by sitting on a young donkey, enacting a piece of prophecy from Zechariah 9:9 that refers to a coming savior who establishes peace over the nations—"Do not be afraid, daughter of Zion. Look, your king is coming, sitting on a donkey's colt!"

So, this is the part of the show with live animals. Jesus rides slowly across stage (or into Jerusalem, as it were) on this donkey, an animal

---

don't need to strive to end poverty. Christians have added a future tense to this present tense statement, translating "you will always have the poor with you" but that interpretation manipulates the meaning of the phrase. This is about Jesus's presence and the importance of Mary's act, not about predicting that we should always expect and accept poverty in this world. I'm looking at you, Christian capitalists!

of peace instead of a war horse. With this action, he accepts the crowds'
invitation to rule. But Jesus, we soon find out, is not a king who has
come to conquer the Romans and win freedom for the Jewish people:
the stakes are much higher and the means of salvation less glamorous.
A group of Pharisees huddle together at the front edge of stage right
and watch the triumphant procession with disdain and fear. They say
to one another, "You see, you can do nothing. Look, the world has
gone after him!" Their words set up the next action on stage, when a
group of Greeks/non-Jewish foreigners approach Jesus to speak to him.
The fact that Jesus's next mini-speeches about salvation are delivered in
response to these Gentiles implies a universality to the salvific descriptions that follow. Through this framing, Jesus's words here continue the
threads of universalism already woven into Israel's Scriptures.[9]

Salvation as Death and Sacrifice

The crowds clear off the stage and the spotlight draws our attention
to Jesus standing on a set of stairs flanked by columns. He makes
an imposing figure—part politician, part sidewalk preacher. "The hour
has come for the Son of Man to be glorified." For the first half of John,
it was not yet Jesus's "hour" but the time has now come. "Very truly, I tell
you, unless a grain of wheat falls into the earth and dies, it remains just
a single grain, but if it dies it bears much fruit." This proverb squelches
the idea that Jesus's kingship on earth will last. He must die for his followers to bear fruit. And who can be his fruit-bearing followers? Jesus
universalizes his salvation with a very Synoptic-like saying: "Those
who love their life lose it, and those who hate their life in this world
will keep it for eternal life." Notice that the hyperbole in his statement
fits well with John's dualistic theme of love/hate and it also creates a different kind of insider/outsider group, one not defined by religiosity
or law-keeping but complete devotion to the kind of life Jesus models.

---

[9] I am thinking especially about the threads of teaching about universal salvation in Isaiah, for example in 25:6–8, 45:22–23, and 53:6.

So it seems that eternal life, that quality of life that Jesus calls them to, does not require a certain ethnicity or religiosity but demands instead self-denial and sacrifice.

Jesus's next words demonstrate courage in the face of sacrifice and fly in the face of the other Gospels' "let this cup pass" garden prayer: "Now my soul is troubled. And what should I say: 'Father, save me from this hour'? No, it is for this reason that I have come to this hour. Father, glorify your name." Jesus shows no uncertainty about his upcoming task, only commitment. The authors of John have taken great pains to portray Jesus as obedient to the Father and in control of his fate throughout the Gospel. Here, we see what might be the Johannine climax of Jesus's authoritative resolve and commitment to God, which contrasts sharply with the other Gospels who portray him as distressed and perhaps even fearful before the cross. It almost feels like John is purposefully responding to the Synoptics' picture of Jesus, as if to say, "Jesus did not turn away from his task, he embraced it." We end up with a *high christology* here—a Jesus who looks more divine than human—while the christology of the garden scenes in the Synoptics is a *low christology*, emphasizing Jesus's humanity. Another difference from the Synoptics is that while Jesus did not get a verbal answer to his plea for the cup to pass, he gets one here. A voice booms from the rafters of the theater, "I have glorified it, and I will glorify it again." Father and son are in lockstep with one another and the audience learns that Jesus is willing and ready to sacrifice his life so that God is glorified.

Salvation as Exorcism

Next, Jesus explains what "this hour" entails and what his death will accomplish. "Now is the judgment of this world," he warns, "now the ruler of this world will be cast out." The word used here "cast out" (*ekballo*) is the same one the Synoptic authors use when they describe Jesus casting out demons. In those Gospels, the authority that Jesus exerts over demons shows his power in the spiritual realm. Jesus has plenty of power in John—he just raised a four-day-dead man from the grave—but he has not performed any exorcisms. The exorcisms in the Synoptics are all part and parcel of Jesus's kingdom-come agenda; they give us a glimpse of God's reign, which will bring physical, mental, and spiritual wholeness. John's plotline doesn't focus on Jesus bringing the kingdom. Instead, it emphasizes that the Son has come to reveal the Father and give life to the world. Part of giving life to the world includes banishing "the ruler of this world," known in John as "Satan" (*satanas*, see 13:27) or "the devil" (*diabolos*, see 6:70; 8:44; 13:2).[10] John uses exorcism language here to demonstrate that although Jesus isn't walking around banishing demons left and right, he will take care of the ultimate evil. How does that work? Let's check back on the speech.

Jesus continues his rousing soliloquy, raising his hands in the air to catch the attention of everyone around him. "And I, when I am lifted up from the earth, will draw all people to myself." Oh, it sounds like the snake on a pole analogy again. But it has acquired even more layers of meaning since we encountered it in the Nicodemus story. By saying he will be lifted up, Jesus is indicating that he will, quite literally, be raised up on the cross and then ascend from the earth into the heavens, AND—like the snake on the pole—people will be drawn to him where they will gaze on their salvation, Jesus's self-

---

[10] The character of Satan has perplexed scholars because its description and function varies so widely in biblical literature and the social context behind the literature. There are also many superstitions and traditions that have fascinated churchgoers throughout history and so scholars have to combat those. Many would agree, though, that "the satan" (*hasatan* in Hebrew; "the accuser" or "the adversary") of Job's introduction and the character who shows up to tempt Jesus in the wilderness (called *satanas* or "satan" in Mark and *diabolos* or "devil" in Matthew and Luke) have some connection, however complicated it might be. Christian tradition often interprets these figures to be the same person throughout the biblical witness, a literal entity known by a host of names: the devil (e.g., Matt 4:1), Satan (used over fifty times), the evil one (Matt 13:19), Beelzebul (Matt 12:24), the deceiver (Rev 12:9), the father of lies (John 8:44), and the ruler of this world (John 14:30). John's portrayal of Satan is complex even within the book, but the representative nature of the character as a personification of evil and evil forces is more apparent in John than it is in the other Gospels.

giving act of love on the cross. Jesus's death will save them, not from snakes in the wilderness, but from Satan, the ruler of the world. The imagery sounds a bit dualistic (and apocalyptic) for our modern minds, but we could say more simply that Jesus will save the world from the evil forces and structures that control our world. That's basically what Satan represents.

According to this speech, then, Jesus's death on the cross will accomplish two salvific acts: draw people to God and cast evil out of the world. A divine hug and a giant exorcism all rolled into one. This also points back to what I said in Act 1 about Jesus's death being apotropaic, or warding off evil. It's pretty clear as the story progresses that Jesus's death on the cross draws people to him because it is an act of utter self-giving love, revealing the character of God to the world. How Jesus's death casts evil out of the world is not so clear. If we stick with the serpent on the pole story for our explanation, then the means of salvation is derived from the source of destruction itself (a bronze serpent heals the people bitten by serpents). That would mean that the means of Jesus's death, an execution by political and religious powers, is related to the destruction from which we are saved—namely, our human enslavement to oppressive powers. In that case, Jesus's death casts out evil by revealing its presence among us and showing us how vulnerable we are to its power. We are saved, then, by *that* revelation along with the expression of God's love through Jesus's life, death, and resurrection, which will draw us to God. Such an explanation does not fit well with the prevailing explanations of salvation in contemporary Christianity, but it does express the message that John's authors seem to be communicating.[11]

Jesus brings his monologue to a close with some images taken from the Prologue and some of his other speeches. Onstage, Jesus's voice takes on a beseeching tone: "The light is in you for a little longer. Walk

---

[11] For those of you who are into atonement theories, John's description of salvation shows us pieces of the Christus Victor, Moral Exemplar, and Scapegoat theories. No Penal Substitutionary Atonement to be found.

while you have the light, so that the darkness may not overtake you. If you walk in the darkness, you do not know where you are going. While you have the light, believe in the light, so that you may become children of light." All the lights on stage fade so the spotlight on Jesus shines even brighter. "I do not judge anyone who hears my words and does not keep them, for I came not to judge the world but to save the world. The one who rejects me and does not receive my words has a judge; on the last day the word that I have spoken will serve as judge, for I have not spoken on my own, but the Father who sent me has himself given me a commandment about what to say and what to speak. And I know that his commandment is eternal life. What I speak, therefore, I speak just as the Father has told me." And with that, the Word has spoken and the audience realizes that they will have to choose light or darkness—receive or reject Jesus—before the drama ends.

CHAPTER SEVEN

Act 4: John 13–20
The Final Countdown

CHARACTERIZATIONS OF JESUS
The Self-giving Servant | The Glorified One | The Spirit Giver |
The Scapegoat

SUPPORTING CHARACTERS
Jesus's mother and the other women | The Beloved Disciple |
Mary Magdalene | Thomas | Peter and the other disciples

Scene 1: The Last Supper (but not the Lord's Supper; John 13:1–30)

Act 4 opens on a meal already in progress, the last one Jesus will have with his disciples. On stage, they are reclining on dining couches, conversing with one another as they eat and drink. It is the night before the Passover festival. The narrator stands to the side of the table, a voyeur at the scene unnoticed by the dinner guests.[1]

---

[1] I have rendered this scene more like a script because it better captures the drama of the chapter in the Gospel. Also, many churches will perform a Last

Narrator: "Jesus knew that his hour had come to depart from this world and go to the Father. Having loved his own who were in the world, he loved them to the end." The narrator walks over to stand behind one of the disciples. "The devil had already decided that Judas son of Simon Iscariot would betray Jesus." *The narrator steps away from the table and allows the scene to unfold from there, uninterrupted.*

Jesus takes off his outer robe, ties a towel around himself, and pours water into a basin. As the disciples look on in horrified silence, Jesus kneels on the dirt floor and begins to wash the disciples' feet, wiping them with the towel that was tied around him.

Simon Peter: "Lord, are you going to wash my feet?"

Jesus: "You do not know now what I am doing, but later you will understand."

Simon Peter: *He jumps up from the floor and backs away from Jesus.* "You will never wash my feet."

Jesus: "Unless I wash you, you have no share with me."

Simon Peter: "Lord, not my feet only but also my hands and my head!"

Supper scene like this on Maundy Thursday during Holy Week and these performances often highlight Jesus washing the disciples' feet (narrated only in John). So, this is also a bit of an homage to those Passion Week skits that have been meaningful to me throughout my years in the church. I pick up the script-like format again later during Jesus's conversation with Pilate because it more effectively conveys the content as an interrogation. Throughout this scene, I have used the NRSVue translation for the dialogue (in quotation marks).

Jesus: "One who has bathed does not need to wash, except for the feet, but is entirely clean. And you are clean, though not all of you." *He raises his eyebrows and gives a pointed look at Judas, but continues to kneel in front of each disciple, one by one, and wash their feet. Once finished, he puts on his robe, returning to the low table.* "Do you know what I have done to you? You call me Teacher and Lord, and you are right, for that is what I am. So, if I, your Lord and Teacher, have washed your feet, you also ought to wash one another's feet. For I have set you an example, that you also should do as I have done to you." *Jesus stands again and walks downstage, aiming his next comment at the audience.* "Very truly, I tell you, whoever receives someone I send receives me, and whoever receives me receives the one who sent me." He turns back to the disciples. "Very truly, I tell you, one of you will betray me."

The other disciples looked at one another, bewildered. Peter motions to the disciple leaning against Jesus, encouraging him wordlessly to say something.

The disciple Jesus loved: "Lord, who is it?"

Jesus: "It is the one to whom I give this piece of bread when I have dipped it in the dish." *Jesus dips the bread and hands it to Judas.* "Do quickly what you are going to do."

ACT 4 PLAYLIST

Scene 1
"Be Our Guest" from *Beauty and the Beast*

Scene 2
"One Last Time" from *Hamilton,*
"SPIRIT" by Beyoncé from *The Lion King* movie

Scene 3
"Trial Before Pilate" from *Jesus Christ Superstar*

Scene 4
"Epilogue" from *Les Misérables*

Scene 5
"History Has Its Eyes on You" from *Hamilton*

Epilogue
"All I Ask of You" from *The Phantom of the Opera*

Narrator: *Speaking to the audience,* "No one knew why he said this to him. But after receiving the piece of bread, Judas immediately went out." *Pausing for dramatic effect.* "And it was night."

The Last Supper scene in John is not a Passover meal; there are no special festival preparations described, as in the Synoptic Gospels. In John, it is actually the night of purification for the feast, which explains Jesus's language about being clean or pure.[2] Also, the meal here does not establish what will later be known as the Lord's Supper: Jesus doesn't break the bread and call it his body, he doesn't pour the wine-blood of the new covenant. But it is still a significant scene for John. Jesus is modeling what life in the community of God should look like when he is gone.

We should notice that the action Jesus performs, an intimate foot washing ritual, comes on the heels of Mary's act of washing and anointing Jesus's feet. It is significant that when Jesus models what service and love of one another look like, he emulates a woman's humble act of devotion to him. Mary's actions stand in direct contrast to those of Peter and Judas in this scene. While Peter resists Jesus's way of service and Judas rejects it, Mary has already fulfilled Jesus's expectations, modeling for all disciples how Jesus serves them and how they should serve each other. In this first-century context, washing someone else's feet was a task for the lowest of enslaved persons because it was a debasing act, as well as a dirty one (walking the dusty roads in sandals equals filthy feet, something I found out when I explored Petra in Chacos). The lowly servanthood inherent in this act, then, was one that few free men would lower themselves enough to do. That Mary and Jesus modeled such degrading humility is significant, both for John's audience and ours.

---

[2] On the night of purification, Jews would often perform sacrifices or wash in ritual baths to achieve ritual purity preceding the Passover feast. John may have mentioned this detail to fit in with his theme of cleansing that continues throughout this passage.

There are other sharp contrasts in this scene. In 13:23, we are introduced to the mysterious figure called the disciple "whom Jesus loved," or the Beloved Disciple. We are told that the Beloved Disciple is reclining close to Jesus's breast (a word often translated "heart"), which is supposed to remind us of the last verse of the Prologue: "No one has ever seen God. It is the only Son, himself God, who is close to the Father's breast, who has made him known" (John 1:18, NRSVue). This description suggests that in addition to Jesus and Mary, this disciple is also an exemplar, someone who mimics Jesus's position in the bosom of God and perhaps makes Jesus known as Jesus makes God known. Conversely, in 13:27, the narrator tells the audience that Satan entered into Judas when he took the bread Jesus offered. One disciple enters Jesus's arms and another has Satan enter into him. The juxtaposition is a warning to the Gospel audience that they will soon have to take sides in the cosmic battle between good and evil. They can choose Judas's path, which leads into the darkness of night or they can be a beloved disciple and stay close to the light of life, even as he goes to the cross.

Scene 2: The Farewell Discourse, CliffsNotes version (John 13:31–17:26)

For this scene, I am going to invoke the playwright's prerogative and trim the narrative down to its salient points. At first read, the passage seems to be an oddly-paced, repetitive mess; there are contradictory exits (see 13:31 and 14:31), awkwardly patched together sayings of Jesus, and a lack of uniformity in content and structure (e.g., teachings about the Holy Spirit/Advocate pop up briefly in chapters 14, 15, and 16, but are never tied together thematically for ease of understanding). However, our contemporary disdain for disorganization may cause us to miss some of the ancient structure woven into the passage. Scholars have noticed that the Farewell Discourse incorporates a variety of ancient genres including testimony (a type of Hebrew literature found in Deuteronomy 34 and the pseudepigraphal *Testament of Abraham*), commission (as in Joshua 1), and consolation literature (in the style of Plutarch's *To Apollonius* and Seneca's *To Helvetica*). The repetitive exits narrated in the discourse look a lot like the "exits to death" found in Greek tragedies such as Euripides' *The Trojan Women*.[3] So, despite its redundancy and patchwork feel, the discourse reflects the influence of popular ancient literature. Maybe not such a mess after all.

For a modern example, scholars have compared George Washington's 1796 "Farewell Address" declaring he would not seek reelection to Jesus's discourse.[4] The song "One Last Time" from *Hamilton* illuminates the parallels; compare "If I say goodbye, the nation learns to move on, it outlives me when I'm gone" (*Hamilton*) to "for if I do not go away, the Advocate will not come to you, but if I go, I will send him to you" (16:7). Taking the various genres represented into consideration, the best way to read Jesus's Farewell Discourse is as a retirement speech in which Jesus reveals truths about his pending exit to the disciples, reassures them in the face of upcoming uncertainty, and gives them high-quality advice about carrying on after his death, resurrection, and ascension.

I have structured the scene as a monologue, so even though the disciples have questions and responses in the passage, the only voice the audience will hear is Jesus's. Some of his soliloquy centers on the key verses from the discourse themes that serve to console and empower the disciples. The rest of Jesus's words (those in italics) will expound on those verses in ways that I imagine Jesus would do if he were speaking to our twenty-first century audience. We have done a good job of twisting many of these discourse sayings and taking them out of context, and I think Jesus might have something

---

[3] See George Parsenios, *Departure and Consolation: The Johannine Farewell Discourses in Light of Greco-Roman Literature* (Leiden: Brill, 2005), 6-7.
[4] See Jo-Ann Brant, *John*, Paideia: Commentaries on the New Testament (Grand Rapids, MI: Baker Academic, 2011), 209.

to say about such misinterpretations. In this part, I am technically going to be putting words in Jesus's mouth (unless otherwise noted), but it is with the noble goal of summarizing a complex, contextual passage and, as always, pursuing responsible biblical interpretation.

Jesus, looking at his disciples and raising his voice passionately: "Little children, I am with you only a little longer...just as I have loved you, you also should love one another. By this everyone will know that you are my disciples, if you have love for one another." (13:33, 34-5, NRSVue)

Jesus, turning to the audience, eyebrows drawn with concern: *I am serious about this. The commandment to love is so central to the character of God and the flourishing of humankind that I am going to lay my life down to demonstrate and exemplify that love. Sure, I have been calling my upcoming death a "glorification" but make no mistake—it will be gruesome and heart-wrenching and it will separate me from you. However, I am willing to endure that if it helps you know that God loves you and expects you to love each other, wholly and sacrificially.*

Jesus, looking at Peter specifically: "Some of you say you want to follow me, that you will lay down your life for me. I am telling you, though before the cock crows, one of you will have denied me three times." (13:36–38)

Jesus, focusing his attention back to the audience: *Don't be so hard on Peter. His heart is in the right place and he's got enthusiasm galore. He just doesn't know himself well. Fear may have overwhelmed him when the heat got too much, but it will not always be the case. Don't be so hard on yourselves either. I love you just like I love him and I will forgive you like I did him.*

Jesus, smiling with encouragement at the disciples and opening his arms wide: "In my Father's house there are many dwelling places. If it were not so, would I have told you that I go to prepare a place for you? And if you say you don't know the way to where I am going, let me remind you that **I am** the way and the truth and the life. No one comes to the Father except through me." (14:2–6)

Jesus, facing the audience and raising his palm in a "wait, a second" motion: But, before you let your mind jump to overly literal interpretations and you use these words to harm or exclude people, let me be clear. I am using the imagery of my Father's house to emphasize that we are a family, not that I am going to pick up my carpenter's hammer and build you a mansion just over the hilltop. When I say I am the way, the truth, and the life, I mean that the example I have lived among you shows you the best way to be human (I am the life) and the words I have spoken will help you know and understand God (I am the truth). It is less that I am opening some cosmic door that God is hiding behind and more that my path in life should become your path (I am the way). Self-giving love and sacrifice, like I have modeled, are the pavement stones on the road to salvation.

Jesus, looking with excitement at the disciples: "Very truly, I tell you, the one who believes in me will also do the works that I do and, in fact, will do greater works than these, because I am going to the Father. I must go away so I can send the Advocate to you." (An amalgamation of 14:12, 16, 18, 28 and 16:7)

Jesus, shaking his head sadly at the audience: This Paraclete or Advocate, the one you know as the Holy Spirit, is the key to this whole endeavor. Yet, so many of you ignore or devalue her importance. You are always wondering what it looks like to do greater works than I did but you will never find out unless you open yourself up to the wisdom, guidance, endurance, and power that comes from the Spirit. As I told *my disciples, I had to go away for the Advocate to come. It is one of the benefits that my death achieves for you.*[5] *So please don't forfeit that gift.*

Jesus, addressing the disciples with a tone of tough love: "I am the vine; you are the branches. Those who abide in me and I in them bear much fruit, but whoever does not abide in me is thrown away like a branch and withers; these branches are gathered, thrown into the fire, and burned...And if the world hates you, be aware that it hated me before it hated you. You do not belong to

---

[5] The spirit, known as *ruach* in the Hebrew (literally, breath or wind), appears in several ways in Jewish Scripture. Sometimes it seems to be a wind with a vaguely divine character (as in Genesis 1:2, when it hovers over the waters) and sometimes it acts as a source of power or authority (as in Numbers 11:16–17 when God takes the spirit upon Moses and shares it with others to lessen the burden of his leadership). In Judges, the spirit shows up to empower the judges when they need it. Climactically, God promises the spirit in Ezekiel 36:26–27: "A new heart I will give you, and a new spirit I will put within you, and I will remove from your body the heart of stone and give you a heart of flesh. I will put my spirit within you and make you follow my statutes and be careful to observe my ordinances." This function of the spirit in Ezekiel has the most in common with the New Testament concept of pneuma, which means spirit, breath, or wind in the Greek (sometimes used by itself and sometimes described as the Holy Spirit). In the Gospels, the spirit is with Jesus during his ministry (e.g. Luke 4:14) and here in John, we get a fuller explanation of the tasks or function of the spirit, especially in this section where Jesus calls the spirit the Advocate (14:26) and the Spirit of truth (15:26) and says that it will remind the disciples of Jesus's teaching and guide them to truth (16:13). In John, Jesus breathes the spirit onto the disciples after his resurrection. In Luke–Acts, the spirit falls on the disciples at Pentecost and remains a central character in the book of Acts, empowering and guiding the early Christians and manifesting in gifts such as tongues and healing. Paul writes often about the spirit as a source of life, empowerment, and unity for believers in his letters, as well as the source of gifts. It is hard to tell exactly how the spirit described in the Hebrew Bible differs from the one portrayed in the New Testament, but the main distinction seems to be that the spirit shows up in specific situations in the HB but becomes more universalized for followers of Jesus in the NT.

the world, but I have chosen you out of the world, therefore the world hates you." (15:5–6, 18–19)

Jesus, smiling knowingly at the audience: I know you have gotten a lot of mileage out of this vine analogy, and I get it, it is a good metaphor. But that's all it is—a metaphor. I used the frightening image of the branches being thrown away and burned to wake my disciples up to the reality that they needed to stick with me and the Advocate through their persecution. I knew that I was not going to be the last person persecuted by the power systems of the world. So, I used this dramatic, dualistic language about fire and not belonging to the world and the world hating my followers as a **persuasive device.** *It was going to be life or death for my followers and I had to prepare them for that. I would appreciate it if you privileged Christians in the back would stop saying the world hates you when you lose a little bit of power in society. That's not what I meant at all.*

Jesus, bringing it home with a prayer for his disciples, and disciples everywhere: "Father, the hour has come; glorify your Son so that the Son may glorify you. You have given him authority over all people, to give eternal life to all whom you have given him. And this is eternal life, that they may know you, the only true God, and Jesus Christ, whom you have sent. I ask not only on behalf of my followers here, but also on behalf of those who trust in me through their word, that they may all be one. Amen, Lord, make it so." (17:1–3, 20–21)

Scene 3: The Condemnation of Crows and Crowds (John 18:1–19:17)

As the lights go down on Jesus's gallows prayer, a ripple of unrest flows through the audience. The darkness of the theater feels different this time, pressing on them like a heavy curtain, threatening to smother.

The stagehands move props off and on stage like shadow walkers; a plaintive melody rises from the pit. It is an oboe, resounding long and low, warning of the tragedy to come. When the darkness on the stage finally abates, we see Jesus and the disciples on one side of the stage and a group of Roman soldiers and police from the chief priests and Pharisee on the other. Judas stands in front of the hostile group, having led them to the garden where Jesus would be. The lanterns the police carry provide the only illumination on the scene. Jesus's voice is the first to slice through the thick air, "Whom are you looking for?"

"Jesus of Nazareth."

"I am he."

The soldiers step back and fall to the ground, knocked over by the force of Jesus's final and definitive "I am" statement. Jesus then demonstrates control over the subdued soldiers with his words, "Fine, if you are looking for me, let these people go." He has quelled the simmering violence and shown that though they have come to arrest him, the whole situation occurs because he has chosen it. On stage, there is an invisible line of separation between Jesus's party and Judas's party, a safe space created by Jesus to protect everyone involved. Abruptly, Peter invades that space and collapses the temporary truce. He draws a sword and swings it with great determination, cutting off someone's ear. It isn't Judas he attacks or even the soldiers. It is an enslaved person from the household of the high priest, the narrator tells us. His name is Malchus. Jesus steps calmly toward Peter, laying a hand on his shoulder. "Put your sword back into its sheath. Am I not to drink the cup that the Father has given me?"[6] (18:11, NRSVue)

---

[6] There are key differences between this arrest scene and the ones in the Synoptic Gospels because John purposely paints a "large and in-charge" picture of Jesus. First, Jesus's "I am" answer that knocks the soldiers off their feet demonstrates Jesus's divine authority and power even as he is arrested. Second, the detail about Peter cutting off the ear of Malchus, highlights Jesus's effectiveness as shepherd and king. Alicia Myers comments that Malchus (which means "king") is left with a deformity here, in contrast to Luke's version in which Jesus heals the ear. That injury shows that the high priest was unable to protect

The lanterns go out as we see Jesus walk away willingly with the arrest party, Peter stumbling along after them, confused and alarmed. It is here that John starts to narrate in alternating story lines—one strand following Jesus to his trials with powerful officials and one following Peter, faced with his own trial by fire.

Peter's not alone as he follows Jesus; "another disciple" is there. That disciple has connections to the high priest, so he is let into the courtyard outside Jesus's impromptu trial.[7] Peter eventually comes into the courtyard as well, thanks to the other disciple's talk with the female guard. The stage is now dominated by two scenes: Jesus being interrogated by the chief priest (stage right) and Peter in the courtyard with a crowd of enslaved people and police (stage left). The spotlight swings to the Peter scene as the woman at the gate does a double-take on Peter: "You are not also one of this man's disciples, are you?" Peter's answer is an anti-"I am" statement: "I am not" (*ouk eimi*). The narrator has to interrupt here to give a detail that will be important in the final scene of the drama. "The slaves and the police had made a charcoal fire because it was cold...Peter was standing with them and warming himself." (18:18, NRSVue)

---

his own whereas Jesus, the shepherd king, uses his words of rebuke to Peter to protect his sheep. Jesus's disciples leave the scene uninjured under his protection. Finally, Jesus's rhetorical question, "Am I not to drink the cup the Father has given me?," reiterates Jesus's resolve to follow the Father's will that we saw in 12:27, and it pushes against Jesus's garden turmoil in the Synoptics. Alicia D. Myers, *Reading John and 1,2,3 John* (Macon, GA: Smyth & Helwys, 2019), 181.

[7] This narrative tidbit about the other disciple (presumably the Beloved Disciple) inspires scholars to find alternate possibilities for the disciple whom Jesus loved. They say it is highly unlikely that John, son of Zebedee (the traditional option for the BD) would have had any connections to the high priest in Jerusalem. According to the Synoptic authors, he was a Galilean fisherman. Lazarus, another possibility for the BD, is more likely to have been known in religious circles in Jerusalem since he was wealthy and lived close to the city. Or, the disciple whom Jesus loved could have been a literary device used by John to encourage his audience to put themselves in the character of the Beloved Disciple.

A beam that resembles an interrogation lamp comes up on Jesus and Annas, the Jewish high priest emeritus. We don't hear the priest's questions about Jesus's teaching but we do hear Jesus's gently sarcastic answer: "I have spoken openly to the world; I have always taught in synagogues and in the temple, where all the Jews come together. If you want to know about my teaching, why don't you ask them?" A figure jumps out from the shadows, the police presence, and strikes Jesus on the face. Jesus rubs his face but replies with cool confidence, "If I have spoken wrongly, testify to the wrong. But if I have spoken rightly, why do you strike me?"(18:23, NRSVue)

The focus returns to Peter, warming himself by the fire. Several of those gathered repeat the female guard's question: "You are not also one of his disciples, are you?" Peter denies it again: "I am not." Someone, whom the narrator tells us is a relative of the man whose ear Peter had cut off, asked, "Did I not see you in the garden with him?" (Implication: weren't you the sword-swinging one?). The audience hears a cock crowing in the distance just as Peter denies his association for a third and final time. Stage left goes dark as the last strains of the rooster's cry fade out.

A light starts to emanate weakly onstage, signaling dawn in the narrative timeline. The action is no longer divided; it's all about Jesus till the end of the scene. We watch as he's dragged by his accusers to the Roman governor's headquarters. Pilate comes out to them because, as the narrator informs us, the Jews wanted to avoid ritual defilement on the Passover (remember, the night of purification they had just completed? Entering into a Gentile space littered with idolatrous images threatened that purity). Pilate barely contains his frustration with the religious men: "What accusation do you bring against this man? Why don't you take him yourselves and judge him according to your law?" The accusers reply, "We are not permitted to put anyone to death." Pilate turns and enters his headquarters, indicating that Jesus should follow him for a private interrogation.

Pilate: "Are you the King of the Jews?" *(Author's note: Pilate asks this hoping to assess the political threat Jesus might pose during the volatile pilgrim festival Jerusalem was celebrating.)*

Jesus: "My kingdom does not belong to this world. If my kingdom belonged to this world, my followers would be fighting to keep me from being handed over to the Jews."

Pilate, growing impatient: "So you are a king?"

Jesus, head raised in quiet defiance: "You say that I am a king. For this I was born, and for this I came into the world, to testify to the truth. Everyone who belongs to the truth listens to my voice."

Pilate, scoffing: "What is truth?"
(Dialogue from 18:33, 18:36, 18:37, 18:38, NRSVue)

The action shifts back outside, where Jesus's fellow Jews are waiting. Pilate's words, "I find no case against him," momentarily ruffle the religious leaders' composure, but Pilate holds up his hand before they can reply. "However… you have a custom that I release someone for you at the Passover. Do you want me to release for you the King of the Jews?" They shout in reply, "Not this man but the rebel Barabbas!"

Pilate leaves the stage and returns with Jesus, but he is placed behind a sheer screen so the audience can see only his silhouette. Soldiers flog him and then place a crown of thorns on his head and a robe on his body.[8] Mocking shouts can be heard behind the curtain—"Hail,

---

[8] Unlike Mel Gibson, the Gospel writers do not linger on the gruesome descriptions of Jesus's torture. The indignity and pain associated with flogging and crucifixion were well-known throughout the Roman Empire, even if it was shameful to write about. John is especially brief in his narration of this scene, perhaps to emphasize Jesus's power in the midst of his weak position, highlighting his composure even as he endures a punishment reserved for enslaved people or those who posed a threat to the empire. That the Gospel

King of the Jews!"—as well as the thud of multiple fist falls. Pilate lines up a set of stairs center stage, obviously preparing for a theatrical tableau. "Look, I am bringing him out to you to let you know that I find no case against him" (19:4, NRSVue). When Jesus is hauled before him, robed in purple and crowned in thorns, Pilate sweeps his hand out like a magician with his big reveal—"Behold the man!"

"Crucify him! Crucify him!" the crowd chants. Pilate shakes his head dismissively. "Take him yourselves and crucify him; I find no case against him" (19:6, NRSVue). The Jews answer him, "We have a law, and according to that law he ought to die because he has claimed to be the Son of God" (19:7, NRSVue). Pilate, looking visibly shaken, pulls Jesus to the side and whispers frantically, "Where are you from?" Jesus remains silent so Pilate taunts him, "Do you refuse to speak to me? Do you not know that I have power to release you and power to crucify you?" (19:10, NRSVue) Jesus replies in a measured tone. "You would have no power over me unless it had been given you from above; so, the one who handed me over to you is guilty of a greater sin" (19:11, NRSVue). The word that Jesus uses here "handed over" (*paradidomi*) appears several times in John's passion narrative. The authors use it ironically. Although many people hand Jesus over—to authorities, to punishment, to death (18:2, 5, 30, 35, 36; 19:11, 16, 30) John portrays Jesus as master over the proceedings, handing himself over to a fate he had already predicted and accepted.

Some people in the crowd, sensing Pilate's hesitancy, interrupt the intimate conversation with a threatening cry, "If you release this man, you are no friend of Caesar. Everyone who claims to be a king sets himself against Caesar" (19:12, NRSVue). Pilate takes the bait and, with the light shining brightly on center stage to indicate the noon hour, he sits on a bench reserved for judgment and addresses the clamoring

---

writers focus on the crucifixion at all shows that they subvert the prevailing idea that dying on a cross signaled weakness and shame. See Jo-Ann Brant, *John*, Paideia: Commentaries on the New Testament (Grand Rapids, MI: Baker Academic, 2011), 155, 232.

crowds. "Here is your king, should I crucify your king?" The mob responds with a cacophonous roar: "Away with him!," "Crucify him!," "We have no king but Caesar." And as Jesus is handed over to crucifixion, the audience remembers Caiaphas's prophetic words from the Lazarus scene, "...it is better for you to have one man die for the people than to have the whole nation destroyed" (11:50, NRSVue). Pilate and the crowd had finally agreed on a scapegoat, but this innocent man would not only save the Jews—he would save all creation.

Scene 4: At the Cross (John 19:18–42)

Throughout this scene, the orchestra is silent. The only sounds onstage are muted sobs from the women disciples and the last words of Jesus when they pierce the eerie silence. It is a pantomime of death. Jesus limps slowly across the stage, carrying his cross. He doesn't falter like in the Synoptics; this Son of God needs no help carrying his cross. Soldiers raise him up between two other victims. The audience has to squint to read the words inscribed over the cross. JESUS OF NAZARETH, KING OF THE JEWS. Soldiers at the foot of the cross huddle together dividing Jesus's clothes up between them. They throw what looks like dice onto the ground for his seamless tunic, callously ignoring the naked body that hangs just above them, slowly succumbing to death.

There are several figures standing near the cross: the disciple whom Jesus loved, the mother who loved Jesus, Mary Magdalene, and another Mary. Jesus speaks. "Woman, here is your son." He tips his chin to the Beloved Disciple then turns his head to his mother. "Here is your mother." The disciple takes the woman's hand in his own. Jesus speaks again. "I am thirsty." Some standing around him soak a sponge in some wine and lift it up to his mouth with a hyssop branch. After it touches his lips, Jesus opens his mouth once more and exhales his next words.

It is finished.

The lights on stage flash, then dim, but not completely. Soldiers walk over to the other condemned men and break legs. When they come to Jesus, they hesitate, sensing there is no life in him. One lifts his spear and pierces Jesus's side. Blood and water gush out. The silence ends with the narrator's disembodied voice: "These things occurred so that the Scripture might be fulfilled, 'None of his bones shall be broken,' and, 'They will look on the one whom they have pierced.'"

Some men appear from backstage, dragging a heavy sack. They approach the cross, take Jesus down, and start to wrap the body in linen cloths. The sharp smell of spices fills the theater. The narrator explains, "Joseph of Arimathea, a secret disciple of Jesus, asked Pilate to let him take away the body of Jesus. Nicodemus, the one who had come to Jesus by night, brought a mixture of myrrh and aloes, so they could wrap Jesus's body according to the burial custom of the Jews. Then they laid him in a nearby garden tomb."

When the narrator finishes his sentence, the curtain begins to close. The rasp of the fabric dragging across the stage is the dominant sound in the room until the two sides meet with a soft sigh. Then, the only noise in the theater is the muted sobs of the audience, trembling and glued to their seats.

Scene 5: The End Was Just the Beginning (John 20)

Before the curtain opens on the final scene, the audience is wiping their tears and full of interpretive questions. I'll anticipate and attempt to answer some of these before we catch up with the Sunday morning visit to the tomb:

- Why did Jesus's mother show up so unexpectedly in the last scene and what is the significance of Jesus's words to his mom and the Beloved Disciple?

- Why did Jesus say, "I am thirsty," and, "It is finished," on the cross when the other Gospels report completely different last words?

- Why do two Jewish religious leaders, Joseph of Arimathea and Nicodemus, get playing time in the crucifixion scene when it was clear that religious leaders were the ones who instigated Jesus's execution?

Jesus's mother appears to bracket either side of her son's ministry, from his first sign at the wedding at Cana to his last breath at Golgotha (in the biz, we call this an *inclusio*).[9] In both scenes, she is an exemplary figure. At the wedding, she trusts in Jesus's abilities and tells people to do what he says—as all followers of Jesus should do. At the cross, she displays courage and fortitude, staying faithfully by Jesus's side despite the danger and heartbreak she faces—as all followers of Jesus should do. When Jesus tells John to take her into his home so they can become family, this is another example for disciples. Jesus's followers (especially the first ones to experience John's Gospel) need to be a community, closer than family, if they want to abide in Jesus's teaching through hardship and persecution. This also makes the Beloved Disciple a paradigmatic figure, representing the ideal disciple who leans on Jesus's breast, follows him into danger, and remains faithful to the end.

Jesus's last words on the cross, although quite different from the Synoptics, are completely consistent with John's narrative.[10] Jesus, the source of living water, the one who causes rivers to flow from

[9] An *inclusio* is a literary device that effectively sets up bookends, or brackets, around a block of narrative to highlight the content in the middle. These might be similar words or characters that show up twice. In this case, Jesus's mother is a model disciple at the beginning of Jesus's ministry and she shows that same commitment at the end.

[10] I realize that my mention of the Synoptics here is quite the teaser and while I'd love to go into the myriad of ways John differs from the Synoptics—and the Synoptics differ from each other—that's a whole other book so I'll leave that to the author of *The Gospels for Normal People* to tackle.

his believers and tells the thirsty to come to him, says, "I am thirsty" before he dies. It is a sad and beautiful irony. When Jesus announces, "It is finished," John is putting the finishing touches on the theme he has emphasized throughout the passion—Jesus is in control of his fate. Jesus has completed the task the Father assigned him, glorification by sacrificial death, and accomplished the salvation of the world.

Finally, the account of two Jewish leaders, Joseph and Nicodemus, taking care of Jesus's body shines a sympathetic light on the group that has been emphatically criticized throughout John's drama—religious leaders. Their part in the story gives hope to the audience that even those who at first reject Jesus's identity as the Messiah can change and learn to trust in the Son of God as Lord.

Now, back to the action. The curtain rises for the last scene and we see Mary Magdalene approaching the tomb, an elaborate set piece dominating the front of the set, stage right. Bright music with a steady beat starts from the pit. Mary sees the stone has been removed, so she turns and runs away. There is a stillness on the stage as the audience waits for what comes next. She returns moments later with Simon Peter and the disciple whom Jesus loved. The music picks up in speed and intensity. The two men race across the stage to the tomb, Peter lagging behind. When they reach the tomb, the prop moves, turning and opening so the audience can see inside. The Beloved Disciple leans in to find Jesus's linen shroud and head cover folded up on the bench. Peter, not to be outdone, goes all the way into the tomb. Both disciples shake their heads in wonder and confusion.

The narrator's voice echoes through the theater as the two men walk away: "The disciples returned to their homes for they did not yet understand the Scripture, that he must rise from the dead." Our focus shifts back to Mary who stands weeping outside the tomb.[11] We watch

---

[11] Elizabeth Schrader suggests the Mary in John 11 who gives the climactic Christological confession could very well be Mary Magdalene. One of her main arguments (along with the conflating of Mary and Martha) is that the traditional translation of Magdalene as someone from Magdala is anachronistic; no village with that name existed in the first century. Instead, Schrader

as she bends to look into the tomb and are just as startled as she is when two angels appear inside. "Woman, why are you weeping?"

Mary Magdalene looks up with tears still streaming down her face: "They have taken away my Lord, and I do not know where they have laid him" (20:13, NRSVue) She turns away from the tomb and the angels disappear into the darkness. A light comes up on center stage and a man half emerges from behind a tree. He addresses Mary: "Woman, why are you weeping? Whom are you looking for?"

The man's face is hidden so the audience cannot see him. Mary begs him, "If you have carried him away, tell me where you have laid him, and I will take him away." The figure steps out fully and the audience recognizes Jesus. "Mary," he says and his voice causes the woman disciple to jump. "Teacher!" Mary's joy is evident in her voice. Jesus takes a step back and says, "Do not touch me, because I have not yet ascended to the Father. But go to my brothers and say to them, 'I am ascending to my Father and your Father, to my God and your God'" (20:17, NRSVue). Mary Magdalene (who will later be known as the apostle to the apostles) runs off stage to announce to the disciples that she has seen the Lord. The stage lights dim.

We should probably pause here and talk about how John's resurrection scenes are noticeably different from those in the Synoptic Gospels. As a reminder, Mark's resurrection appearance is actually a non-appearance. The women disciples come to the tomb on Sunday morning, hear the message from the man dressed in white, then run away in fear saying nothing to anyone (the original version of Mark ends right there, in 16:8). Matthew's version is similar, although the women do tell the disciples in that narrative, and then Matthew ends his Gospel with the story of Jesus commissioning the disciples (you know, "Go and make disciples of all nations..."

---

posits that Magdalene is a title, translated "the tower," and that Mary the Tower is John's Peter the Rock. Mary the Tower gives the key confession at Lazarus's tomb and now meets Jesus at *his* tomb to become the apostle to the apostles.

see Matthew 28). Luke elaborates even more on Mark's account, adding the charming story about the two disciples walking to Emmaus who meet Jesus but don't recognize him (like Mary doesn't recognize him here!). In Luke, Jesus also appears to the disciples, tells them to touch him to prove he isn't a ghost and then eats fish with them like a flesh-and-blood human. Luke ends with Jesus's ascension, which is not included in Mark and Matthew's Gospels.

John has a total of four resurrection appearance scenes: Jesus meeting Mary Magdalene near the tomb (we just experienced that one), Jesus appearing to the disciples to give them the spirit, Jesus appearing again to reassure Thomas, and then the miraculous catch of fish/reinstatement of Peter scene in chapter 21 (that was probably added by later editors). There are some parallels between John's scenes and the Synoptics: women (or one woman) are the first witnesses to the resurrection in all four Gospels. Jesus eats fish with his disciples in both Luke and John, although in different settings. And Jesus commissions the disciples in Matthew, a scene that may parallel Jesus's reinstatement/commissioning of Peter in John 21. Yet John's stories remain quite distinct and that is probably because John's authors have some storylines to tie up. Jesus spoke enough about the Holy Spirit in the Farewell Discourse that we need some closure around how and when he left that spirit with the disciples. The scene with Thomas ends up being a great way to incorporate the first hearers of John into the story—they may not have seen Jesus but they believe and are blessed for it (or maybe they doubted and are absolved for it). The final scene, which focuses on the future discipleship of Peter and John, also connects to John's audience, explaining the fates of and relationship between two of the key disciples—Peter, whose legacy had a significant impact on the early church and John, whose discipleship had some unrecoverable connection to the writing of John's Gospel. It is important as we witness these last scenes from John that we think like the original audience and try to experience what they would have experienced through this curious and dramatic end to the Gospel.

The lights come up and the scenery has changed. The disciples are huddled together in a room with adobe-colored walls. They look fearful because of the message they had received from Mary. Jesus strolls casually on stage as if he hadn't just died and risen from the dead. The audience erupts in applause. "Peace be with you." He says this to the disciples and the audience. He points to his hands and his side and the disciples start laughing nervously, the kind of laughter born from a tense situation, half anxious, half relieved. Jesus quiets them, "As the Father has sent me, so I send you."

Then Jesus breathes on the disciples: "Receive the Holy Spirit. If you forgive the sins of any, they are forgiven them; if you retain the sins of any, they are retained" (20:23, NRSVue). The audience is as confused as the disciples until it dawns on them that Jesus said he had to go away for the Advocate to come. Jesus is making good on his promise to leave them his power. For those of us familiar with Luke's account of the early church—Acts—we may be concerned that the giving of the Holy Spirit occurs at Pentecost there and not in a private room with Jesus like it does here. The result is the same—the believers receive the spirit—but John seems to want that to occur in a setting that is more communal and personal, at a time when Jesus is still around. So, when did the spirit actually come? Well, that would be asking a modernist question of an ancient text and we have learned not to do that, haven't we?

The disciples leave the stage and the scene changes. A spotlight moves to stage left where a single disciple stands alone. The other disciples emerge from the wings. "We have seen the Lord," they all say to Thomas. Thomas narrows his eyes, gauging whether they are pranking him. He can't decide, so he just says, "Unless I see the mark of the nails in his hands and put my finger in the mark of the nails and my hand in his side, I will not believe" (20:25, NRSVue). They all move offstage as the lights go down.

When the audience looks back, the scenery has not changed but it is clearly a different day. Jesus appears out of nowhere and delivers his favorite post-resurrection line: "Peace be with you." Thomas is there and Jesus addresses him, "Put your finger here and see my hands. Reach out your hand and put it in my side. Do not doubt but believe" (20:27, NRSVue) Thomas falls to his knees and cries, "My Lord and my God!" (20:28, NRSVue)

"Have you believed because you have seen me?" Jesus walks forward to address the audience. "Blessed are those who have not seen and yet have come to believe" (20:29, NRSVue) The house lights come up.

The narrator starts to cross the stage to Jesus, speaking as he walks: "Now Jesus did many other signs in the presence of his disciples that are not written in this book" (20:31, NRSVue). The narrator stops next to Jesus and looks into the faces of the audience members. "But these are written so that you may come to believe that Jesus is the Messiah, the Son of God, and that through believing you may have life in his name" (20:31, NRSVue). The curtain closes. The audience starts to clap but the curtain opens before they can stand. Apparently, the show's not over yet.

The Epilogue (John 21)[12]

The orchestra starts to play what sounds like a bar tune, softly at first, but growing in volume as the scene progresses. Apparently, there's one last musical number before the story comes to a close. A screen is lowered from the rafters. There are no actors on stage but a scene starts to flicker on the screen as if an old filmstrip was running through a broken projector. It looks like a twentieth-century Jesus film, complete with low-budget special effects and cheesy Bible-times costumes. A group of fishermen are in a boat, throwing out their nets. There is no sound

---

[12] You may have noticed the end of John 20 seemed like the conclusion of the Gospel. John 21, according to scholars, functions like an appendix and was likely added to the Gospel later, perhaps to explain the legacies of the apostles Peter and John (if John is, indeed, the Beloved Disciple). I have separated it from the rest of the story to illustrate this literary history.

from the film yet. The time lapse suggests that they fish all night but every time they pull up the nets, they're empty. The sun rises behind the tired men and then the camera zooms in on a lone figure walking up the shore. The mystery man calls out, "Children, you have no fish, have you?" The men in the boat yell back, "No!"

"Cast the net to the right side of the boat, and you will find some" (21:6, NRSVue). The men throw out the net; when it comes up, it is teeming with fish. The fishermen strain to pull it in. The youngest man turns to an older man and exclaims, "It is the Lord!" The audience fills in the blanks on this fragmented movie scene. The young fisherman is the Beloved Disciple. The older one is Simon Peter. Peter throws on his outer garment and jumps into the sea. The other disciples guide the boat with the miraculous haul back to shore.

The camera angles in on Jesus, who is sitting by a fire cooking fish and bread. "Bring some of the fish that you have just caught," he says encouragingly. Peter goes to the boat and hauls the net ashore, still intact and full of large fish. Jesus waves everyone over: "Come and have breakfast." Jesus takes the bread and gives it to them and does the same with the fish. After they finish their meal, Jesus turns to Peter: "Simon son of John, do you love me more than these?" Jesus gestures to the other disciples. The film Peter looks suspicious but answers, "Yes, Lord; you know that I love you." Jesus replies, "Feed my lambs."

The music from the pit shifts into a minor key, mid-song. Jesus asks again: "Simon son of John, do you love me?" Peter answers impatiently, "Yes, Lord; you know that I love you." Jesus curtly nods his head, "Tend my sheep." The disciples around the fire are starting to whisper to one another. Jesus inquires a third time, mirroring the three times Peter denied him during the passion scene: "Simon son of John, do you love me?" Peter's eyebrows knit together and he hunches over as if the words had punched him in the gut, "Lord, you know everything; you know that I love you." Jesus says,

"Feed my sheep."[13] Jesus stands up and starts to walk down the beach, beckoning Peter to follow.

The camera follows them as Jesus leads Peter away from the other disciples. "When you were younger, you used to fasten your own belt and to go wherever you wished. But when you grow old, you will stretch out your hands, and someone else will fasten a belt around you and take you where you do not wish to go." The orchestra hits a sour note. "Still, you should follow me." The camera shot widens and we can see the disciple whom Jesus loved following them. Peter looks a little shell-shocked when he gestures to that disciple, "Lord, what about him?" Jesus's tone turns sharp: "If it is my will that he remain until I come, what is that to you? You just need to follow me!" The camera pans out on the beach and the narrator voice-over starts. "So the rumor spread among the brothers and sisters that this disciple would not die. Yet Jesus did not say to him that he would not die, but, 'If it is my will that he remain until I come, what is that to you?'" (21:21, NRSVue)

The picture grows staticky again and the sound fades out. Words appear on the screen, superimposed over the beach scene. They read: *This is the disciple who is testifying to these things and has written them, and we know that his testimony is true. But there are also many other things that Jesus did; if every one of them were written down, I suppose that the world itself could not contain the books that would be written.* (21:24-25, NRSVue)

---

[13] There has been debate about this passage when it comes to the verbs translated as "love" in 21:15–17. The author switches between the verb *agapao* (used in Jesus's first two questions) and *phileo* (used in his third time) and some commentators (especially preachers!) find various hidden meanings in the change. Most scholars have noticed, however, that John's Gospel uses the two verbs interchangeably. They deny that there is a special meaning to the switch in verbs. The main point in these verses is not found in the verb switch but in how many times Jesus asks Peter if he loves him—the three times signals earnestness and echoes the three times that Peter denied Jesus in 18:15–25. See Alicia D. Myers, *Reading John and 1, 2, 3 John: A Literary and Theological Commentary* (Macon: Smyth&Helwys, 2019), 210.

The orchestra plays a final note with a flourish and the curtain closes. The audience jumps to their feet in a standing ovation and their applause fills the theater until the curtain call begins. During the curtain call and even as the audience files out to return to their lives, the question that John's drama posed over and over again lingers in their minds.

"Will you trust that Jesus is the Messiah, the Son of God, and find life in his name?"

CHAPTER EIGHT

So What?

Thank you for journeying through this dramatic presentation of John's Gospel with me. You have been an open-minded and adventurous audience, and I thank you for trusting me as we found a new way to experience John together.

You might have noticed that I ended the Epilogue with a line from John that sounds like an altar call. That was intentional but I assure you, I am not trying to dredge up traumatizing memories of singing all the verses of "Just As I Am" at a revival service. I am not an evangelist calling for you to walk the aisle and pray the sinner's prayer.

John, however, was an evangelist, at least of the first-century variety. And one of the main goals of this Gospel was to inspire the audience to react to Jesus's story, to help them come to an understanding of who Jesus was (the Messiah and Son of God, John writes), and consider how they might trust Jesus and receive the life he offers. That invitation is what I have tried to replicate in my reimagination of John and that is what I hope you have experienced—an inspiring and life-giving story that calls for a response, whatever that might be for you.

After I attend a moving musical or watch a particularly thought-provoking movie, I don't want to get up and go back to the real world immediately. I want to sit for a while, allow the last notes of the music to reverberate in my body, let all the thoughts and feelings I have experienced wash over me, or maybe even turn to my companions to talk about the plot twists or the breath-taking performances.

I hope you will do that with John. This story was meant to be experienced, fully and viscerally. It was meant to linger in our retrospective solitude and be shared in our communities, discussed with people who see beauty and truth a little differently than we do. So, I hope you let this story sit with you and I hope you share it with others. And one more thing...

May the God who loves the world and sent the Son give you the kind of life Jesus offers, that abundant and eternal life that gushes like a spring of water and becomes a river for those around you (John 3:16, 4:14, 7:38, 10:10, 17:3).

AMEN.

Things for Normal People to Read (Or Not... No Judgment)

Alter, Robert. *The Art of Biblical Narrative*. New York: Basic Books, 1981.

Bauckham, Richard. *The Testimony of the Beloved Disciple: Narrative, History, and Theology in the Gospel of John*. Grand Rapids, MI: Baker Academic, 2007.

Beirne, Margaret. *Women and Men in the Fourth Gospel: A Genuine Discipleship of Equals*. JSNTSup 242. Sheffield: Sheffield Academic Press, 2003.

Brant, Jo-Ann A. *Dialogue and Drama: Elements of Greek Tragedy in the Fourth Gospel*. Peabody, MA: Hendrickson, 2004.

Clark-Soles, Jaime. *Scripture Cannot Be Broken: The Social Function of the Use of Scripture in the Fourth Gospel*. Leiden: Brill, 2002.

Coloe, Mary L. *Dwelling in the Household of God: Johannine Ecclesiology and Spirituality*. Collegeville, MN: Liturgical Press, 2007.

Conway, Colleen M. *Men and Women in the Fourth Gospel: Gender and Johannine Characterization*, Society of Biblical Literature Dissertation Series 167 (Atlanta: Society of Biblical Literature, 1999).

Gench, Frances Taylor. *Back to the Well: Women's Encounters with Jesus in the Gospels.* Louisville: Westminster John Knox Press, 2004.

Kittredge, Cynthia Briggs. *Conversations with Scripture: The Gospel of John.* Harrisburg, PA: Morehouse Publishing, 2007.

Koester, Craig R. *Symbolism in the Fourth Gospel: Meaning, Mystery, Community.* 2nd ed. Minneapolis, MN: Fortress Press, 2003.

Kysar, Robert. *John, the Maverick Gospel.* Rev. ed. Louisville: Westminster John Knox Press, 1993.

Lincoln, Andrew T. *Truth on Trial: The Lawsuit Motif in the Fourth Gospel.* Peabody, MA: Hendrickson, 2000.

Myers, Alicia D. *Reading John and 1, 2, 3 John: A Literary and Theological Commentary.* Macon, GA: Smyth & Helwys, 2019.

Reinhartz, Adele. *Befriending the Beloved Disciple: A Jewish Reading of the Gospel of John.* New York: Continuum Academic, 2002.

Ringe, Sharon H. *Wisdom's Friends: Community and Christology in the Fourth Gospel.* Louisville: Westminster John Knox Press, 1999.

Schneiders, Sandra M. *Written That You May Believe: Encountering Jesus in the Fourth Gospel.* Rev. ed. New York: Herder & Herder, 2003.

Segovia, Fernando F. *The Farewell of the Word: The Johannine Call to Abide.* Minneapolis, MN: Fortress Press, 1991.

Skinner, Christopher W. *Reading John.* Eugene, OR: Wipf and Stock Publishers, 2015.

Voorwinde, Stephen. *Jesus' Emotions in the Fourth Gospel.* Harrisburg, PA: Trinity Press International, 2005.

About this Book

About the Author

Jennifer Garcia Bashaw (PhD, Fuller Theological Seminary) is Associate Professor of New Testament and Christian Ministry at Campbell University in North Carolina. She is an ordained Baptist minister and has a passion for teaching the Bible and training pastors. Jennifer is a Nerd-in-Residence for the Bible for Normal People and is the author of *Scapegoats: The Bible through the Eyes of Victims*.

Behind the Scenes

Publishing Director Lauren O'Connell
Cover Design Tessa McKay Stultz
Layout Designer Ania Lenihan

Special thanks to the eagle-eyed members of our Society for Normal People community who read through the final draft of the manuscript and provided feedback, caught spelling errors, and generally ensured we don't look like fools: Michael Burdge, Bonnie Hardin, Richard Healey, Brian Hutzell, Christina (Chris) Jackson, Frances Nelson, Clint Redwood, John Shumate, Peter Wall, and Katherine Wharton. We couldn't do what we do without you.

Enjoyed this Book?

To continue the conversation, head over to thebiblefornormalpeople.
com where you can:

- Listen to The Bible for Normal People and Faith for Normal
  People, the only God-ordained podcasts on the internet.
- Join our online community, the Society of Normal People,
  where you'll get access to members-only content and perks,
  and journey alongside others.
- Find even more books written by biblical scholars for normal
  people, just like you.
- Enroll in one of our online classes.
- Pick up some exclusive B4NP merch.

Or follow us on Facebook and Instagram (@thebiblefornormalpeople)
for more Bible for Normal People content.